IMPACT

IMPACT

A Functional Curriculum Handbook for Students with Moderate to Severe Disabilities

by

RICHARD S. NEEL, PH.D.

and

FELIX F. BILLINGSLEY, PH.D.

College of Education
Experimental Education Unit
University of Washington

·P A U L·H·
BROOKES
PUBLISHING CO.

Baltimore • London • Toronto • Sydney

Paul H. Brookes Publishing Co.
P.O. Box 10624
Baltimore, Maryland 21285-0624

Typeset by Brushwood Graphics, Inc., Baltimore, Maryland
Manufactured in the United States of America by
Thomson-Shore, Inc., Dexter, Michigan.

Library of Congress Cataloging-in-Publication Data
Neel, Richard S.
    Impact: a functional curriculum handbook for students with
moderate to severe disabilities/by Richard S. Neel and Felix F.
Billingsley.

        p.   cm.
    Bibliography: p.
    Includes index.
    ISBN 1-55766-026-3
    1. Handicapped children—Education—United States—
Handbooks, manuals, etc.   I. Billingsley, Felix F., 1942–
II. Title.
LC4031.N425   1989
371.9'0973–dc20   89-7114
                                                          CIP

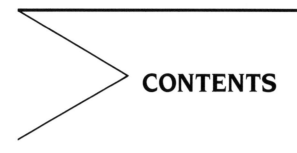

CONTENTS

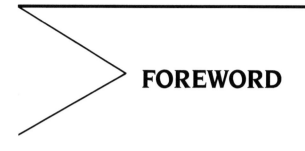

FOREWORD

It was not until the early 1960s that children with autism and other moderate to severe developmental disorders became students for the first time. Until the pioneering efforts of a handful of behavioral psychologists in the United States and Great Britain during the 1960s, autism was a label that ensured a great deal of diagnostic attention and clinical curiosity but little in the way of meaningful intervention that would improve the lives of the children given this label and their families. Stimulated by advances in learning theory—and perhaps a bit bored by further demonstrations of learning by laboratory animals—these early behavioral scientists were determined to show that the "new" laws of behavior and learning principles could be applied to serious human needs. Hence, laboratory classes, schools, and even group homes were supported by these professionals at major research universities in North America and Europe. In these special environments, university professors and their students were dedicated to teaching children with autism and other developmental disorders to learn and do things they had thus far been unable to achieve.

The structure of such settings remained fairly constant for a long period of time. Children and youth were selected for enrollment on the basis of their diagnosis—such as autism—and were organized into small classes, in which the primary mode of instruction was one professional (or parent or trainee) working with one child at a time. The format of the early learning experiments with laboratory animals was adopted virtually unchanged as the format of instruction for children with disabilities, and the "discrete trial" was widely endorsed as the most appropriate model for teacher-pupil instructional interactions. The tasks that were to be learned by these first students were selected based upon developmental considerations but also the requirements of the instructional situation. First, children and youth with mental retardation and autism were often assessed as being "developmentally young," so that their instructional objectives were selected from a continuum of skills more appropriate to much younger children matched according to constructs such as "mental age" without regard to chronological age. Second, as the discrete trial format typically involved child and teacher seated facing one another—sometimes with and sometimes without a table in between—it was perhaps predictable that many of the tasks learned in these settings were things like puzzle assembly, ring stacking, bead stringing, identifying colors and shapes, tracing letters, and pointing at and labeling body parts and pictures. These were all the sorts of things that could be done at tables while seated on chairs, over and over again until the child "got it right." Similarly, the principles of learning were individually applied to design effective rewards for appropriate responses and punishments for inappropriate ones. And, again, the classroom setting, the one-to-one teacher-child dyad, and especially the discrete trial format, virtually dictated that the range of possible rewards and punishments was also restricted to the set of relatively artificial consequences that could be delivered in such a situation. Thus, tokens and candy and praise would be given for correct answers, and not given or even taken away for incorrect answers or inappropriate behavior.

This work did give us the earliest evidence that these children not only could but would learn when provided with systematic attention and the expectation that they perform. Such evidence was a major contribution in the history of both educational psychology and developmental disabilities. The interest in identifying causes of autism and mental retardation and preventing future cases has continued, but the technology of educational intervention has grown remarkably in sophistication since those first laboratory classes in the 1960s. Parents now have more to look forward to than only the hope for a future cure, as education provides direct support to assist *people* with autism and other moderate to severe disabilities to become meaningful participants in society—even as these very real people may continue to carry such diagnoses with them throughout their life spans. We can be grateful to the pioneers who left the far more controlled environment of the animal laboratory and were willing to take on the challenges of children and their families. But at the same time, it is time to confront the limitations of this early work and move on to the more demanding challenges of assisting children and their families *in their neighborhood schools, natural homes, and local communities.*

The fact that the theory describes a predictable chain of behavior and we can design a discrete trial to model such a chain in practice should not condemn us and the children we teach to school careers, personal interrelationships, and a lifestyle dictated by a series of commands and consequences to shape the performance of meaningless tasks in artificial situations and "special" environments. Basic scientists need not concern themselves with much more than the immediate demands of the experiment. In contrast, applied scientists, such as educational and psychological researchers—who work with people—must by definition deal with multiple sources of influence, unintended effects, and the social as well as the experimental validity of each intervention. Clearly, our task is a difficult one, but as the old adage states, "No one ever said it was going to be easy."

The IMPACT curriculum has its roots in applied behavior analysis and systematic instruction, but leads us into the next generation for students with severe disabilities. IMPACT incorporates the scientific clinical approach represented by early work in behavioral psychology and special education, but integrates science and clinical practice into the context of the natural environment. As before, systematic instruction and data-based performance decision-making form the core of the curricular approach. But the choice of curricular goals is shaped not only by the current level of functioning of the child, but by his or her age as well. The procedures specified in the IMPACT curriculum assist professionals and caregivers in identifying those age-appropriate functional skills that are critical for the needs of the individual child. In addition, our attention is directed to the many dimensions of the life of the school that provide invaluable learning contexts for children. For example, much has been written over the years about the difficulties that children with autism have dealing with transitions and changes in their world, and, in the past, programs have been designed to protect these children from learning to cope with such changes. In contrast to these past practices that actually increase the gap between the coping skills of children with disabilities and their peers, the IMPACT curriculum shows parents and teachers how to view and use transitions as important instructional opportunities.

The materials represented in this volume acknowledge and value the full participation of these young people in life at school, in their families, and in their communities, and in meaningful interactions with their peer group. Guidelines for individualizing instruction in typical situations and settings are the essence of IMPACT. The IMPACT curriculum does not depend upon an expectation that caregivers and intervention professionals can control "outside" sources of environmental influences. Instead, the emphasis is upon instruction carried out in the context of natural environmental events—the daily routines of everyday life. This means that the stimulus for the child's behavior must be the natural environmental cue or event that typically guides behavior. Similarly, naturally occurring consequences and corrections must be utilized to motivate the child with autism or other developmental disabilities just as is the case for other children. Thus, the IMPACT curriculum does not require that a child's lifestyle be compromised as the environment is stripped of meaning and purpose in the guise of instructional control. On the contrary, education should build upon the powerful motivators that already exist in schools, neighborhoods, families, and peer groups, and services delivered should not rob children of their right to be part of their communities. The kind of integration of science and practice represented by the IMPACT curriculum provides an outstanding model for the next step in our efforts to meet the needs of persons with moderate to severe disabilities in a manner that does not sacrifice their quality of life in the process.

Luanna H. Meyer, Ph.D.
Syracuse University
Syracuse, New York

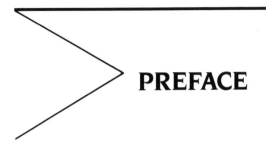

PREFACE

One of the most significant accomplishments in education over the past several years has been the inclusion of children with moderate to severe disabilities in public schools throughout the country. Those children, who were historically not a major responsibility of schools, are now being served by public schools throughout the nation. In fact, in most communities, the public school program may be the major service children with moderate to severe disabilities and their families receive. It is imperative that educators provide the best possible service. This handbook is addressed to the parents, teachers, and other professionals who are involved in the development and/or implementation of quality programs. Our overriding purpose in writing this handbook is to provide an integrated curriculum from which such programs can be developed.

The order of the handbook follows the logical sequence that would be used in developing a program for a child with moderate to severe disabilities. Part 1 beings with an overview of the handbook and recommendations for its use (Chapter 1). Next, the goals of the curriculum are presented (Chapter 2), followed by a brief discussion of functional curricula (Chapter 3), and the major assumptions of IMPACT (Chapter 4). We believe that the ability to communicate is a skill of fundamental importance for all children; therefore, in Chapter 5 a thorough discussion of language and communication is provided. For individuals who have had little experience with the language and communication skills of children with moderate to severe disabilities, this chapter should be studied in detail. Those with more thorough training or greater experience in language and communication will find Chapter 5 a concise refresher. Part 2 examines the assessment process using both the Home and Community and the School and Community inventories (Chapter 6). Setting priorities and writing truly functional individualized education programs is the subject of Chapters 7 and 8 respectively. Once goals have been written, Part 3 of the handbook shows how to develop the instructional process (Chapter 9). Special topics, such as teaching in context (Chapter 10), behavior problems (Chapter 11), and alternative responses to behavior problems (Chapter 12) are given special treatment because they often appear to be particularly troublesome for educators. The final chapter (Chapter 13) shows examples of daily schedules for elementary and secondary classrooms. This chapter also includes suggestions about integrating instructional programs for more than one child and for children with different disabilities.

The handbook also includes four helpful appendices. Appendix A shows blank versions of all the forms that appear throughout the handbook for use in assessment and instruction. Appendix B shows the IMPACT Home Inventory, which is used to assess individual child needs in the home environment in terms of where the child goes, how well he or she communicates, and how well he or she handles changes. Appendix C shows the IMPACT School Inventory, which is used to assess individual child needs in the school environment in terms of where the student goes, how well he or she communicates, and how well he or she handles changes. Appendix D is the Parent Guide, which helps parents understand the approach and process of IMPACT, in addition to their role in IMPACT. Appendices B, C, and D are also available as separate booklets to facilitate use of the IMPACT curriculum. Ordering information can be obtained from Brookes Publishing Co., P.O. Box 10624, Baltimore, Maryland 21285-0624.

The IMPACT handbook does not contain lists of skills that ought to be taught in a number of curricular "domains." Rather, the chapters outlined above describe a comprehensive set of procedures designed to identify those skills that are relevant to the needs of each pupil, promote instructional practices that are consistent with those needs, and be useful across children who vary widely in both current ability and apparent motivation.

ACKNOWLEDGMENTS

The ideas in this handbook have many roots. As in all team efforts, the authors only claim the impetus for starting the project and the tenacity for seeing it to completion. The ideas and procedures developed in this handbook are the result of the efforts of many people. Certain individuals, however, played a major role in its development and deserve special mention. We would like to acknowledge Deborah Symonds and Frances McCarty. They helped nurture the beginning ideas, and this project would never have been started without their continual prodding and support. We would also like to thank Cathy Lambert, Nancy Smith, Rae Hanashiro, Donna Bergerud, and Michael Boer for their valuable input into the various parts of this book. Thanks are also due to Luanna H. Meyer for all the help she has given throughout the development of this curriculum. Her insights were accurate and well-timed, and delivered with warmth and support. She has played a major role in shaping the ideas found in the handbook. Finally, we wish to express our appreciation to Melissa Behm at Paul H. Brookes Publishing Company for her continued interest in two reluctant authors.

IMPACT

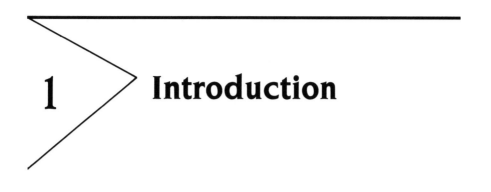

1 Introduction

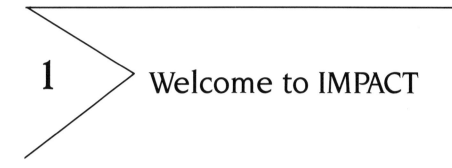

1 > Welcome to IMPACT

Welcome to the IMPACT curriculum handbook. This handbook is designed to provide you with the tools necessary to design, implement, and monitor an effective functional school program for children with moderate to severe handicaps, including severe mental retardation and autism. IMPACT is a different type of curriculum, and this handbook is different from most that you may have read in the past. IMPACT is a highly individualized curriculum based on the functional intents of each student. Since many of the functional goals of children with moderate to severe handicaps are idiosyncratic, different techniques of assessment and instruction will have to be utilized. Classroom design and schedules will need to be altered to accommodate the functional programs you develop. In other words, by using the IMPACT curriculum you will not only change what you teach, but how you teach as well.

The IMPACT handbook is designed to meet the needs of novices and experienced parents and educators. As noted above, implementing a functional curriculum will require that everyone involved in providing a quality education for children with moderate to severe handicaps learn new skills and develop a different view of what an effective school program should look like. This handbook was developed to help you in that process.

1. The chapters in Part I of this handbook make up the "Introduction," which provides background for those who are new to functional curricula. Some of the notions and terminology used may be foreign to you. In addition, many of the methods of determining goals, writing individualized education programs (IEPs), assessing performance, and providing instruction will be different from other curricula with which you may be familiar.

We have written this first chapter to explain how to use the handbook. "What Is Impact" discusses the goals of the curriculum and how the program integrates traditional services and activities into a different instructional format. A discussion of the benefits of a functional approach along with a brief history of instruction for children with moderate to severe handicaps are covered in "Introduction to Functional Curricula." The primary assumptions that underlie the techniques used in this handbook are discussed in "IMPACT's Assumptions." "Language and Communication: A Primer on Programming with Pragmatics" is designed to provide you with the understanding necessary to effectively integrate communication instruction into your programs. We believe that communication skills and the social interactions that come from them are the most important skills anyone can learn. This chapter is very important and should be read thoroughly.

2.   If you are ready to set up (or convert to) a functional program, then you can skim "Welcome to IMPACT," "What is IMPACT," and "Introduction to Functional Curricula." However, read "IMPACT's Assumptions" and "Language and Communication" carefully before you go to Part 2, "Getting Started."

Part 2 covers the process for designing a functional program, enlisting the support of other persons involved, and developing the instructional activities and materials needed to provide an effective program for children with moderate to severe handicaps. Special attention is given to involving parents in every step of the process. You will be able to follow the procedures detailed step-by-step, from setting up a program to documenting performance. For those who have an existing program, tips are given to help you plan for a smooth transition to the new curricula (see Chapters 8 and 9).

The steps provided can be followed as presented, or they can be modified to meet your special circumstances. The curriculum is flexible enough to accommodate the special needs of the children you teach, the individual requirements of your educational settings, and, of course, your own teaching style. Modifications that have been tried in various classrooms are highlighted throughout the text.

The actual process of instruction, including especially troublesome problems, are covered in Part 3, "Learning with IMPACT." Often the general case described does not fit the particular needs of one of your children. Part 3 is designed to provide you with specific skills to use IMPACT as well as an in-depth treatment of special problem areas. Exceptions to the general rules as well as various modifications of suggested techniques are covered. One point to remember is that whenever you make a change, be sure to maintain the functional aspects of each instructional program. It is the reliance on the functional process that ensures success of the curriculum.

3.   If you have an existing functional program and are looking for specific solutions, then the handbook can be used as a reference book. Educating children with moderate to severe handicaps is difficult. Many existing programs with experienced staff run into problems. Several different problem areas are discussed and the handbook is referenced by topic area in the index. Techniques are covered at the introductory and advanced level. Experienced teachers will find many helpful suggestions on how to refine their programs and how to develop solutions for the difficult idiosyncratic problems children often present. The reference list provides information for for further study.

The IMPACT handbook can be used in a variety of ways. As you become familiar with its contents, you will find it to be a valuable tool in helping you plan and implement an effective program.

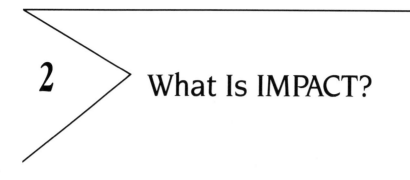

2 > What Is IMPACT?

IMPACT'S GOALS

The goals of the IMPACT functional curriculum are: 1) to increase participation of each student in various environments, 2) to increase the degree of influence each child has over the events that affect him or her, 3) to allow the development of functional school programs within integrated public school settings, 4) to provide assistance in the development and implementation of a continuing partnership between students, parents, and teachers for the education of children with moderate to severe handicaps.

1. IMPACT is designed to teach the skills that will enable each student to participate more effectively in various home, community, and school environments. It is designed to increase effectiveness in current situations and to develop access to additional environments that will be beneficial throughout each child's lifetime.

2. Children with moderate to severe handicaps often have a great deal done for them or to them. They are frequently not allowed to express their preferences or act on their own. IMPACT programs focus on developing functional skills in natural environments so that the degree of influence each child has over his or her own life is increased. We have found that this increase in independence maintains the skills taught in the program.

3. In order for children with moderate to severe handicaps to effectively participate in normal adult environments when they grow up, they will need to be educated in settings that include a broad range of children. Since several of the elements of the IMPACT curriculum are different from those generally used in traditional classrooms, careful attention is given to the integration of the curricula into regular school settings.

4. For an educational program to be maximally effective it must have the cooperation of all persons involved. Children need to be able to integrate their needs into the curricula. Parents will want to provide vital information as to the goals of the instruction and the overall effectiveness of the learning. Teachers and other school personnel will provide much needed expertise in the areas of assessment, program design, instruction, and evaluation. The effective integration of all this information into a cooperative educational program provides the fundamental structure of the IMPACT curriculum.

IMPACT CURRICULUM FEATURES

Ensuring the effectiveness of the IMPACT curriculum makes the following curriculum features essential:

> Individualizing the instruction according to the functional intents of each child
> Integrating traditional services into a functional instructional program
> Teaching skills that are critical to maintain effective participation in the least restrictive environment
> Teaching skills to a level of proficiency necessary to maintain them after instruction is finished
> Teaching skills that increase the number and types of environments that the child can participate in, especially independently
> Teaching skills that influence life in nonschool environments
> Evaluating instruction in terms of actions in nonschool settings

CURRICULUM STRUCTURE

When you use IMPACT it will provide you with the basis for selecting functional instructional programs for each child within your classroom. It will give you the means to systematically assess and prioritize the skills needed to contribute significantly to the ability of your students to adapt to multiple environments and situations, and thereby participate more fully at home, in the community, and at school. It does not contain a collection of specific tasks broken down into their component parts, nor does it provide a developmentally sequenced listing of skills through which each of your children should proceed. Although task analyses are certainly valuable tools to the successful instruction of many handicapped learners, and lists of developmentally sequenced skills may provide a familiar basis for the selection of teaching objectives, neither is sufficient to adequately serve the need of pupils with moderate to severe handicaps. A reliance solely on training in developmentally appropriate forms of behavior frequently results in the functional aspects of an activity being ignored.

This handbook also presents an instructional system that teaches skills in context so that the child's performance will be brought under the control of natural cues and consequences. This focus on appropriate instructional context results in pupils learning skills that are most critical for them. Once acquired, skills taught in one set of contexts often generalize to similar situations without further instruction (Billingsley and Neel, 1985).

THE INSTRUCTIONAL PROCESS

There are three major phases in the IMPACT instructional process: 1) goal setting and IEPs, 2) assessment, and 3) instructional programming.

Goal Setting and IEPs

Traditionally, goals have been based on where the pupil tests in relation to the development of nonhandicapped children. In a developmentally sequenced curriculum, the instructional milestone becomes the next step in the developmental sequence. This continues until, presumably, the pupil has mastered the prerequisite skills to achieve some future outcome. In contrast, in the first phase of the IMPACT curriculum, instructional priorities are taken from the child's environment. When determining which goals to teach, you need to know which environments a student participates in and to what degree he or she can function independently within those environments. You will also need to know how many environments your students have access to. If a student has access only to school and home, then you will want to develop programs that increase the number of environments available to that student. There are Environmental Inventories in the handbook to help you collect this critical information.

The Environmental Inventories tell you what skills a pupil has in several areas, how many environments he or she participates in, and the degree of supervision and assistance required to maintain the student in each setting. These inventories become the basis for writing the IEPs. They will help you and the parents come to an agreement regarding which skills to teach and in what order they should be taught. They will also help you decide which particular contexts to utilize during instruction, who will be doing the teaching, and when the program will take place.

Using the Environmental Inventories to formulate your instructional goals provides several benefits. First, since the skills taught are selected from current environments, they will be able to be used as they are taught. This will enable each student to profit from the immediate utility of the instruction. Second, the opportunity for each new skill to come under the influence of natural cues and consequences is increased and the chances that, once learned, the skill will be maintained are improved. Third, instructional goals are unique to each individual. This gives you an instructional program that focuses on the current needs of each pupil rather than on his or her performance on a test on various developmental milestones.

Assessment

The second phase of the IMPACT curriculum is assessment. In traditional curricula, assessment consists of determining how well the student performs in several developmental domains (e.g., fine motor, gross motor, language) in an artificial classroom or test situation. Each skill is measured in a context where it would not normally be used. IMPACT assessments measure skill sequences (routines) within natural contexts. These sequences, if performed correctly, produce something for the student. For example, the purpose of preparing a snack is to get something to eat. A functional assessment in this context, then, measures a student's ability to perform the steps necessary to obtain food. In order to ensure that the skill is being measured in a context in which it is likely to be required again, the assessment is done during snack time. The degree and types of assistance required to ensure success are also measured. This information is then translated into an instructional program.

By measuring skills in the context where they will be used, you determine what types of instruction will be necessary to increase a pupil's ability to successfully participate in different environments. A developmental assessment tells you which milestone is next; however, this provides little information concerning the pupil's performance in natural settings. If you are unable to determine which milestone will have an effect in the natural setting, it is tempting to choose the next step along the continuum of normal development as your next instructional target. Often this leads to programming that focuses on temporary or nonfunctional skills. The functional assessment process prevents these problems.

IMPACT includes a system for selecting the appropriate context for instruction as well as techniques for assessing your student's current level of performance across different contexts, environments, and skill areas. Assessment forms are used to pinpoint the level of functioning across selected goals, and this information leads directly into the instructional programming process.

Instructional Programming

In many curricula designed for children with moderate to severe handicaps, teaching consists of a series of programs in each of the developmental domains, scheduled throughout the day. For example, language ("points to picture of food items") is from 10:00 to 10:30, and dressing ("zips zipper on Raggedy Andy") from 10:35 to 10:50. For each domain (fine motor, gross motor, language, cognition, and social), growth is measured by how many correct responses are given on each program and by the number of steps mastered along the various continua. Growth measured in this way is often illusionary. The increases in behavior often disappear when the instruction has ceased, and what seems like progress often fails to provide the child with useful skills in any permanent sense. For a skill to be meaningful to a student, it must be used in natural situations. Learning an isolated skill, or even 1,000 isolated skills, is not necessarily growth in a meaningful way. Functional instructional programming, the third phase of IMPACT's curriculum, is designed to teach useful skills in natural contexts to increase the student's ability to participate in those contexts as learning progresses. The promise of future effectiveness is replaced by the demonstration of current effectiveness.

Functional instructional programming entails designing an instructional sequence (routine), selecting the instructional context, teaching, collecting information (data) on the effectiveness of the teaching, and then making the necessary changes indicated by the data. Many changes will take place when you implement this curriculum in your classroom. You will not, for example, be able to schedule language programs from 10:00 to 10:30. You will provide instruction in each skill, instead, when and where it would normally be required. For example, to teach a pupil to dress independently, instruction will be scheduled in places where there is a reason for changing clothes. Instead of having 10 or 20 trials of "pants on" and "pants off," you will develop dressing routines that precede gym, follow gym, precede swimming, and so forth. Parents will also be encouraged to follow similar routines changing clothes at bedtime and when their child gets up in the morning. Each opportunity to instruct in dressing will only be done when it is necessary for the pupil to change clothes. Likewise, language programming will occur when the child needs to communicate, and eating, when he or she needs to eat. Skills will be taught in integrated units. This will result in fewer programs because for many skills that traditionally have been separated, instruction will be provided in one functional routine.

IMPACT's goals are to increase the overall influence of children with moderate to severe handicaps over the events of their lives. This is accomplished by developing an alliance between the child, his or her parents, and school personnel. The instructional process is based on the determining of functional intents of each child in a variety of natural environments. These intents are then prioritized by the parents and teachers to form the IEP for each child. Then the performance level of each child is assessed by measuring his or her ability to complete functional routines in natural settings and under nontraining situations. Instructional programs are then created to increase their independence in these settings. This process provides an instructional program that is functional and truly individualized.

3 ▷ Introduction to Functional Curricula

The goal of this curriculum is to enable children with moderate to severe handicaps to participate in their environments to the maximum degree possible through improved communication and independence. To do this, a fundamental change in the teaching environment is required. Basic to this change will be the understanding and acceptance of new standards for what constitutes a good program. All of us have been accustomed to evaluating success in terms of milestones achieved and/or elimination of undesired or disruptive behaviors. A great many of the instructional curricula developed thus far are predicated on this model. The IMPACT curriculum is based on a functional model. It teaches children with moderate to severe handicaps skills that enable them to increase their influence over the events of their lives. As their influence increases, so will their independence. It is this combination of increased influence and independence that characterizes the IMPACT model.

A major focus of the IMPACT curriculum is the development of communication skills that are needed in the child's home, school, and community as part of an integrated instructional package. Communication skills are the most important skills any child can learn. IMPACT integrates the teaching of communication skills into all of its instructional programs. This ensures that the communication skills are learned along with the other functional skills in situations that require those skills in the natural environment. This integration of skills from all domains into one behavioral routine helps ensure that the student will reach his or her desired outcomes.

The change to a more functional curriculum is founded on the belief that the developmental model's view of success is illusionary and not always in the best interest of the child with moderate to severe handicaps. Radical changes in the expected educational outcomes are required if we are going to improve the quality of the lives of the children we teach. A brief summary of the development of education programs for children with moderate to severe handicaps will help explain what changes are needed and why.

HISTORY OF PROGRAMMING FOR
CHILDREN WITH MODERATE TO SEVERE HANDICAPS

The application of behavioral technology to the education of children with moderate to severe handicaps has produced a drastic change in school programs. Ferster (1961), Gold (1973), Horner and Bellamy (1979), Lovaas (1965, 1968, & 1973), and others demonstrated that children with moderate to severe handicaps could learn skills that would enable them to participate more effectively in society.

Once the educational technology of how to teach was demonstrated, the question of what to teach became a major concern. For many, the initial issue was not curricular content, but providing programs for their children in public schools. PL 94-142, the Education for All Handicapped Children Act of 1975, had ensured a free and appropriate education for all children, and early efforts focused on providing those programs. The need for curricular content became apparent as programs were developed. What should we teach children with moderate to severe handicaps? Naturally, educators looked at what nonhandicapped children did for the answer. This was predicated on the belief that children with moderate to severe handicaps learn like other children, just at a slower pace. The stage theories of Piaget (1947) and Gesell and Amatruda (1949) became the major building blocks of developmental curricula. Most programs consisted of lessons in fine and gross motor, cognitive/preacademic, communication, self-help, and social domains. Tests were developed to measure progress along each of those, or similar developmental continua (e.g., Bendersky, Edgar, & White, 1977). Instruction became a series of isolated developmental sequences taught through forward chaining. Many of those sequences were linear, vertical approximations of normal development hierarchies. In short, the educational programs for children with moderate to severe handicaps became systematic, smaller steps through the same developmental milestones as children without handicaps. It soon became apparent that the soundness of using such sequences to alter the effective functioning of children with moderate to severe handicaps was not verified (Brown et al., 1979).

Unfortunately, there was not enough time allowed to teach all the skills that would be needed. Teaching technologies were then developed to increase the efficiency of instruction and accelerate the pace with which children with moderate to severe handicaps could progress through the curriculum; however, as instructional efficiency increased, more developmental domains were included in the curriculum. As programs developed and children moved through the specified skill sequences, it was discovered that the skills learned were, in many cases, nonfunctional (Brown et al., 1979). Tasks taught were often just the exemplars of various concepts measured by developmental tests. The specific instructional skills were not age-appropriate, nor were they likely to be useful throughout the majority of the child's life. Many of the skills that were taught would require advanced proficiency to be functional. Some stunning examples make the point. For noun identification, children were taught to point to a plastic doll and rubber ball. Evidence of the concepts of protestation and negation were identified using programs involving Yes and No responses, with forced choices between cookies and vinegar. Communication was taught through the repeated requests, "Look at me" and "Show me eat" and "Show me drink" during snack time. Academic programs designed to teach the reading of words, filling in the hands on a clock, and solving simple math problems became widespread. Such programs were abandoned as children reached adolescence in favor of more vocational tasks because the children had not reached a level of fluency that would allow them to use the skills effectively in nonschool environments. For many, the time remaining to learn all the skills necessary to function successfully in independent or supported work settings was far too short.

Progress was made in programs for children with moderate to severe handicaps. Children who were previously excluded were in school and learning new things. They were being trained to "act normal" in school settings. Growth in real terms, however, was rarely measured. Growth, in and of itself, became the standard of a successful program, regardless of whether or not that growth made any real difference in the child's ability to participate in his or her environment. To be sure, some growth appears better than no growth. Getting better at the wrong things, however, is not getting better. A change in approach was needed.

As more data were collected on the effectiveness of instruction, the focus of parents and teachers shifted to the quality of programming provided. The outcome of developmental programs was that children with moderate to severe handicaps were indeed in schools, and they were learning tasks, many for the first time; but they were not substantially better off as adults. The end result, institutionalization and isolation, was only postponed. The utility of the developmental tasks had passed before individuals were able to use them. What was being taught resulted in 20-year-olds functioning like 4-year-olds. Much of what had been demonstrated in the classroom disappeared in other settings. Enthusiasm about growth toward developmental milestones waned. The illusion of progress was slowly challenged by parents and teachers.

Developmental program demonstrations did, however, serve a useful purpose. They demonstrated that children with moderate to severe handicaps could learn and that they could be educated in public schools. They provided the basis for further curriculum development and convinced educators that providing an effective education was well within their grasp.

As the awareness of the difficulties of developmental programming grew, work on other models began. The functional curriculum model used in IMPACT is the result of these efforts. Chapter 4 outlines the assumptions underlying the IMPACT model.

4 ⟩ IMPACT's Assumptions

IMPACT is based on six assumptions that are interwoven throughout the curriculum and that form the underlying theoretical framework. Below is a brief description of each assumption and what impacts each has on the development and design of the curriculum.

1. *Increasing control over the environment is the major goal of instruction.* When you do not have many skills, it often seems that things are always done to you. Children with moderate to severe handicaps often throw temper tantrums out of frustration due to their inability to communicate their needs or understand what others expect of them. As children develop functional skills, they increase their ability to influence what happens to them. IMPACT is based on the belief that instruction should focus on enabling children with moderate to severe handicaps to participate in their environments to the maximum degree possible through improved communication and independence. It is this focus on selecting only those skills that contribute to increased influence and independence that distinguishes IMPACT from more traditional curricula.

2. *Communication/social skills are the most important skills a child can learn.* Communication/social skills are not independent of their contexts. Words and acts separate from their implied intent have little or no purpose. The language programs of the early 1970s have clearly demonstrated that the apparent growth in speech and language is not necessarily growth in communication (Lovaas, 1973). IMPACT is grounded in the belief that children with moderate to severe handicaps need to be taught to communicate using a wide variety of communicative forms. It is the act of communication, not simply speech, that enables them to influence the quality of their lives. Additionally, communication/social skills need to be taught where they will be used. If children are going to communicate effectively, they must learn to get their message across in real situations. This is markedly different from teaching a specific language form in a structured classroom communication or language lesson scheduled for one hour three or four times a week, and then asking the child to try to correctly apply what he or she has learned to another situation. All of us use a complex set of communication tools to gain understanding. It is no different for children with moderate to severe handicaps. If we want these children to gain any modicum of success in controlling their environment, we must teach them to communicate in settings and situations that matter to them, and cease the practice of teaching them to "talk like me" in isolated classroom settings.

3. *Motivation is achieved by ensuring that instruction produces desired results for the student.* Frequently, children with moderate to severe handicaps seem to have such difficulty in learning that elaborate, artificial reward systems are employed to promote learning. Far too often, the growth demonstrated by such systems is fleeting. This is due in part to the selection of instructional targets that produce limited or no increase in influence or independence for the learner. When we attempt to teach skills that are not functional for a student, artificial rewards are required to develop and maintain them. In order to promote skill acquisition and maintenance, the IMPACT curriculum relies on the reinforcing properties of achieving a desired goal. We believe that for a skill to be useful, and therefore a legitimate candidate for inclusion in an instructional program, it must be an integral part of a series of activities that will produce results desired by the child. It is the IMPACT philosophy, therefore, that every activity and skill that needs to be taught can, and should, be integrated into a routine leading to a critical effect for the child.

4. *Functional skills are best taught in their natural context.* Functional skills are those skills that are frequently required in a child's environment to produce a desired result. White (1980) calls this result the critical effect of a behavior. The idea of a functional curriculum is to focus on teaching each child how to reliably produce the effects he or she desires. Some examples of effects a child might need to produce are having enough to eat, protesting, contacting others, having fun, keeping warm, getting from one place to another. The IMPACT curriculum is based on the belief that such functional skills should be taught in natural contexts. Teaching in context removes much of the generalization and motivation problems that occur when teaching is done in settings that are contrived or only remotely resemble the actual settings in which the behaviors will have to be used. Since teaching occurs in environments that a child would normally frequent and where a desired effect is more likely, he or she exerts more control over the environment and is more motivated to learn the tasks required. Additionally, the student is more likely to use the skill the next time he or she returns to this environment. The natural cues and consequences that will control and maintain a skill sequence are learned during instruction, so additional generalization training is often either not necessary or shorter in duration (Billingsley & Neel, 1985).

A child will frequent many different types of environments. Sometimes the skills needed in one environment cannot be easily taught in another. There are even times when skills required in one environment are likely to inhibit learning skills required in another. Take, for example, the skills of sitting in your seat and raising your hand before entering a conversation in a classroom. Those skills are considered necessary by most teachers to maintain an orderly learning environment. They are, however, not skills used in a family or community setting. In fact, learning to raise one's hand may inhibit learning the more subtle aspects of turn-taking required to carry out a conversation in a nonstructured setting. Whenever such conflicts occur, priority has to be given to home and community tasks. The goal of any curriculum should be an improvement in the quality-of-life for children with moderate to severe handicaps in all environments. One key to this goal is promoting effective participation in natural settings. Thus, it is important that skills taught are those that allow the child to function in community settings and win the approval of significant others (Koegel, Rincover, & Egel, 1982). Life long skills taught in enduring environments form the basis for the instructional design of the IMPACT curriculum.

5. *Instructional priorities come from the individual and his or her environments.* Curriculum targets can be drawn from many different sources. Traditionally, they have come from

the development of nonhandicapped children. Functional curricula take their instructional goals from the desired outcomes of each individual. It is this reliance on the desired outcomes that makes the IMPACT curriculum truly individualized. For instructional routines to be effective, they must lead the student to a desired outcome. Therefore, instruction must be based on the desired outcomes of each student.

Many desired outcomes can be reached in various ways. It is crucial that the skills taught to achieve a particular outcome be effective in the various environments that the child has access to. A setting for the desired outcome to be able to play outdoors without supervision, for example, needs to be available at the time of instruction. Your student will need to have several outdoor play areas that usually do not have regular supervision available if this skill is to be taught. You cannot expect your student to learn this skill by learning to play independently in the classroom or on highly supervised outings. If no appropriate places exist, access to such places will have to be developed *at the time of instruction*, or the instructional goal will have to be altered. To be effective, the specific skill or routine taught to reach a desired goal must be one that can be used in current environments throughout the instructional process.

6. *Parent participation is the crucial component of the instructional process.* Parents are an essential and integral part of every step in the IMPACT curriculum. They have the greatest investment in their child's growth and adjustment to society and possess the requisite knowledge of what skills the child must learn to have an impact on his or her environment. As Schopler (1976) says, "Parents have the strongest motivation for rearing their child effectively and within the range of their own life-styles. In fact, they have the greatest potential for being the primary experts on their own child, for understanding the child's learning levels, and forming realistic expectations for his future" (p. 240).

Besides providing crucial input about their child's functioning, parents can become valuable working members of their child's educational team. Parents can provide information available nowhere else. They know which environments their child currently has access to and will determine to a great extent the future environments available to their child.

Information on desired goals of each student are often known only to parents and siblings. This information is critical to effective instructional planning. Without accurate knowledge of desired functions and available opportunities within the student's environment, effective programs cannot be developed. Valuable time will be lost designing and implementing spurious programs and dealing with the behavior problems they produce.

Koegel and his colleagues (Koegel et al., 1982) suggest that close cooperation with parents is essential in increasing the availability, intensiveness, and cost-effectiveness of the education of children with autism as compared with direct clinical treatment. They suggest that parents can provide a valuable source of direct measures of the children's behavior, as well as measures of parent-child interactions. Our experience is that this is true for parents of all children with moderate to severe handicaps.

If a curriculum is to have a positive impact, it is critical that the problems of generalization and maintenance be addressed. This necessitates the involvement of parents in their child's education. Lovaas (1973) found that the children of parents trained in program management continued to improve, while those children returned to nontrained parents or to institutions lost the gains they had achieved through intervention. Hence, if we are to reach our goal of improving the quality-of-life of children with moderate to severe handicaps, parents must be involved in the curriculum.

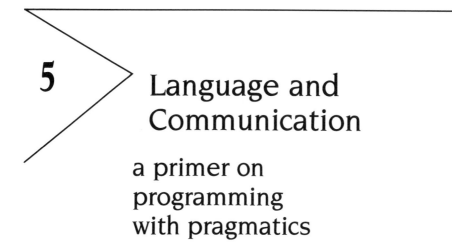

5 Language and Communication

a primer on programming with pragmatics

LANGUAGE CURRICULA

A major problem that children with moderate to severe handicaps have is their inability to effectively use communication to control their environment. In the past, instruction in language skills for these children has been provided in isolation. Using behavioral techniques, researchers have demonstrated how they could be taught various skills in structured educational settings. Once it was demonstrated how to teach, it became necessary to determine what to teach. To date, a majority of the content of language training programs for children with moderate to severe handicaps has consisted of teaching toward normal developmental milestones. The expectation for such programs was that when the basic skills of normal language development were mastered, the children then could be taught more advanced skills, and ultimately they would learn a useable language system. Unfortunately, this does not happen.

Language curricula based on normal developmental milestones are usually split into two separate categories: expressive and receptive language skill training. Expressive and receptive language skill training programs are very similar in content. The major difference is that expressive programs provide training in spontaneous initiated language use, whereas receptive programs provide training in the understanding of language.

Expressive language targets usually include tasks like labeling objects, activities, and parts of speech; requesting behaviors; or greetings. To build on these basic expressive skills, children would then be taught the next series of skills in the sequence of normal development. If a child learns to label a ball using the word "ball" in response to the question, "What is it?", the next step is a two-word label such as, "a ball" and then, "It's a ball." Similarly, if a child requests a cookie by saying "cookie," the next instructional target might be, "Want cookie" and then, "I want cookie."

Receptive skill training usually includes tasks like discriminating names of objects, activities, and parts of speech; responding to simple commands; recognizing different sounds; and responding to one's own name. This kind of language training should result in children acquiring a comprehensive language system similar to that used by nonhandicapped peers.

Segmenting language training programs for children with moderate to severe handicaps into sequential steps resembling normal language development has had less than favorable results, due in part to a discrepancy in acquisition rates. Acquisition of language skills occurs at a very rapid pace in the nonhandicapped population. Unfortunately, however, the acquisition rate of new skills is so slow for children with moderate to severe handicaps that traditional language programs have resulted in children learning only bits and pieces of the total picture. The communication systems that are acquired are generally inadequate and unusable in natural environments.

The settings selected for traditional language programs were based on results of laboratory studies that demonstrated the effectiveness of behavioral techniques. A typical class consisted of a teacher and child seated at a table with only those materials relevant to a particular language task. Emphasis was placed on minimizing extraneous variables and cues that might interfere with the child's ability to attend to the "correct" discrimination. Both physical (irrelevant materials, classroom activity) and verbal (irrelevant cues, classroom noise) distractions were limited. Using these behavioral techniques, under very controlled conditions, some children with moderate to severe handicaps acquired basic expressive and/or receptive language discriminations. The success of these language programs was usually supported by classroom data demonstrating that when the child is given a standard set of cues, he or she performs the task to preset criteria during instructional programming.

Such progress provides a false sense of accomplishment. While classroom data often suggested that children with moderate to severe handicaps learned a variety of language skills through instructional programming, their inability to communicate outside of the training setting remained unchanged.

This lack of generalization to situations and people outside of the training setting is due in part to the use of inappropriate content as well as irrelevant contexts in which the skill instruction was provided. Inappropriate content refers to the discrepancy between program content and those skills that are required in daily life. In other words, the teacher provides training in skills that the child does not have an opportunity to use in mainstream environments. Context irrelevancy, on the other hand, refers to the restructuring of classroom settings so that they no longer resemble the natural environment. For example, the teacher trains a child in language skills at a table from 10:00 to 10:25, minimizing physical and verbal distractions, and creating an artificial or severely limited social context. The end result of training inappropriate content in an irrelevant context is that children with moderate to severe handicaps fail to learn when and where to use acquired skills. It does not matter whether a child learns 5 or 500 nouns; if he or she does not know when or where to use them, the skill learned is useless.

The failure of existing language programs to produce generalized communication skills has forced educators to consider alternate communication skill training strategies. "Children learn to communicate through parent-child interactions in which real conversation, real requests for attention and assistance, real question asking and answering are carried out . . . children learn to communicate in a social context in order to make changes in their environment. This would seem to suggest that the most effective method of teaching communication skills would involve instruction in natural environments in the context of purposeful activities" (Nietupski, Schuetz, & Ockwood, 1980, p. 22).

The trend toward training in the natural environment is reflected in the emergence of functional communication skill instruction. Functional skills are those skills required of the child in his or her natural environments. The more frequently a particular skill is required, the more functional that skill becomes for the child. When the child receives training in those skills that he or she has an opportunity to use, program content becomes appropriate for that child. Training in skills that can be directly applied to real situations provides the child with a way of increasing his or her participation in the environments.

Appropriate content is often determined by the situations (context) in which the child uses each communication skill. Different situations require different skills. Consequently, educational programs must also attend to the relevant contextual features (physical, temporal, and social) surrounding all skills taught. Including relevant contextual features in each instructional program for the child with communication needs provides training in when and where to use each acquired skill. Generalization is inherent in each program.

The IMPACT curriculum emphasizes training in functional communication and social skills in naturally occurring situations. Appropriate program content and relevant contexts are determined by parents and teachers through the Home and Community and School and Community Environmental Inventories which are discussed in Chapter 6 (see Appendices B and C). Once the content is selected, communication instruction occurs throughout the school day within a sequence of purposeful activities. Those activities are naturally occurring routines the child completes throughout an ordinary day at school, at home, and in the community. By utilizing relevant contextual features and training in appropriate content, teachers can maximize the communicative potential of children with moderate to severe handicaps.

THE FUNCTION OF COMMUNICATION

The goal of each communication program is to increase the ability of children to influence and participate in natural environments, using communication. To realize this goal, communication programming must include teaching a response mode (form) that is effective in producing changes (functions) for the child across situations. Regardless of the form used, if the child's communicative intent increases the control he or she has over the environment, then that communication is functional for the child.

To develop functional communication programs that address these goals for children with moderate to severe handicaps, both communication functions and forms must be considered. A comprehensive program must assess the communication functions a child currently utilizes in the natural environment and the forms used to meet each function. Training emphasizes building an increasing number of functions as well as shaping new forms, or increasing the sophistication of existing forms. The greater the number of functions a child can utilize to satisfy a variety of interactions, the more communicative control he or she will have. Concurrently, having a variety of forms available will increase the child's ability to utilize the functions that are intact.

Before developing a communication training program that will teach children to use acquired skills to control their environment, several concepts must be considered. These include the difference between language and communication, what it means to be a competent communicator, how communication operates in the environment, and how form is used to satisfy communication functions.

Language and communication are terms that are frequently used interchangeably. However, the ability to use language is very different from the ability to communicate. Language refers to the use of an organized set of symbols like the spoken word, whereas communication encompasses a much broader spectrum of behavior. Children who are unable to use a set of linguistic symbols may be able to adequately communicate. Many children with moderate to severe handicaps fail to develop an adequate language system. In the population of persons with autism, children who have fairly complex language or complicated symbol systems may still fail to use them communicatively. The IMPACT curriculum focuses on the ability of children with moderate to severe handicaps to communicate with others regardless of their ability to use language. The following paragraphs describe what it means to be a competent communicator.

Competent communication is achieved through the ability to act as either the speaker or the listener within a given context. As a speaker, this includes the ability to use a communication system or form (e.g., talking, signing, gesturing, pointing to pictures) to influence the attitudes, beliefs, or behavior of the listener. To influence the listener in a desired manner the speaker must produce a spontaneous communication within a given situation to which the listener may respond (Lucas, 1980). This requires having communicative intent and signaling it to the listener. In addition, the speaker must be able to use any relevant contextual cues that may enable the listener to accurately understand the message. If a child intends to tell an adult he or she would like additional milk with dinner, stating "more" may not provide enough information for the message to be understood. Holding up the empty cup while saying "more" utilizes the relevant contextual cues to convey the intended message.

Fulfilling the listener's role requires the ability to recognize or understand the speaker's intent and respond accordingly within the same context. In the above example, for the adult to fulfill the listener's role, the message for more milk must be understood and either accepted or rejected to be considered an effective communication.

It is not necessary to have an elaborate language system to be an effective communicator. Any behavior that successfully expresses the intention of one person toward another is a communication. Children who are preverbal successfully demonstrate different language functions using gesture and vocalization to communicate specific intent. Children with verbal skills use more sophisticated language forms to serve the same functions.

Normal Communicative Functions

Before an adequate communication program can be designed, it is necessary to determine the specific function of a particular communication. The following functions occur in normal language development and express the variety of functions communication serves:

1. ***To Satisfy Material Needs or Wants*** Satisfying material needs or wants is typically exemplified by requests, which may be verbal or nonverbal. Children who are nonverbal may point to what they want or pull you to a specific area. Children with limited verbal skills may label a desired item or use incomplete sentences. Children who are verbal usually use some form of an "I want" statement. Any behavior that is understood by the listener and consistently produces a desired object or activity for a child successfully demonstrates this function.

2. ***To Protest*** The ability to protest provides children the opportunity to refuse or reject an undesirable object or activity. Children who are nonverbal or preverbal typically demonstrate protest by using gestures. This includes clenching their teeth together when being fed, pushing an offered item away from them, or wiggling away from an activity and failing to cooperate in a daily routine. Children with limited verbal skills use the word "no" to protest any undesirable object or event. Children with greater verbal skills can protest by stating, "I don't want that," "I don't like it," "I don't want to play," and so forth.

3. ***To Exert Control over the Environment and over the Behavior of Others*** While all communication skills provide children with a certain amount of control over the environment, exerting control over the environment and over the behavior of others is used specifically to affect the behavior of others within the environment. Children who are nonverbal may use behaviors like dropping a cookie over the edge of the high chair to watch an adult pick it up. Children with limited verbal skills may label an activity and guide an adult through it, such as stating "up" and pulling an adult out of a chair, or "down" and sitting the adult down again. Children with more sophisticated verbal skills can exercise this function by commanding specific behaviors such as, "Come with me," "Stand up," and so forth.

4. ***To Establish and Maintain Contact with Important Persons in the Environment*** Establishing and maintaining contact with important persons in the environment is accomplished when the main intent of any communication is to establish and sustain social contact with people important to the child. Children who are preverbal may use repetitive vocalization such as babbling to further this intent. Children with limited verbal skills may use conversation topics that have been successful in the past at maintaining social contact. For instance, such a child may refer to a particular toy or game that usually encourages an adult to play with him or her. Children with greater verbal skills utilize this function in conversations where implied "me" and "you" phrases are used, as in talking about an event that both parties have in common.

5. ***To Express Individuality and Self Awareness*** In expressing his or her individuality and self-awareness, the child intends to gain personal acknowledgement as an entity separate from others in the environment. Any communication that is intended to call attention to the child and gain recognition fulfills this function. Children who are preverbal may use acting out behaviors like doing cartwheels in a group of adults or laughing loudly during a conversation. Children with limited verbal skills may label an activity to call the adult's attention to what he or she is doing. Children with more sophisticated verbal skills use statements like, "Watch me," "Here I come," or "See what I can do."

6. ***To Ask about the Environment*** Any communication that results in additional or novel information and increases the child's understanding of the environment addresses the child's need to ask about the environment. Children who are preverbal may hold up an item and look at an adult to request a name for it. Another preverbal form that demonstrates this function is repetitive pointing to objects in a room as an adult labels them. Children with limited verbal skills may say "What's that?", while children with more sophisticated verbal skills express their intent with statements like, "Tell me why" or "Tell me about that."

   7.   To Play Act or Pretend   An extension of gaining novel information is the child's ability to create unique situations using a variety of communication forms. The content of this pretending may be things never personally experienced or previously experienced situations that are rearranged in a novel manner. Preverbally, this may be accomplished by acting out situations, for example, feeding dinner to dolls or dressing in someone else's clothes. Early verbal pretending may include talking about personal experiences using different characters. Children with more sophisticated verbal abilities fulfill this function by using language to create imaginative stories.

   8.   To Communicate Experiences Not Shared by the Listener   A child who can communicate experiences not shared by the listener allows the listener to have symbolic participation in the experiences of another. The speaker builds on his or her ability to use a language system and knowledge of his or her relationship with the listener to relay information that has not been shared by the listener. This function also requires attending to relevant contextual cues of the experience that must be included for the information to be easily understood. To effectively communicate unshared experiences it is important for the speaker to respond to cues that indicate that the listener does not follow what is being said. Successful use of this communication function depends on the speaker's ability to adjust the amount or content of shared information.

Communicative Functions for Children with Moderate to Severe Handicaps

Many children with moderate to severe handicaps clearly have severe communication problems. While the basic functions listed above cover normal communication development, many of those functions can be better assessed in children with moderate to severe handicaps if they are separated into different, more practical, distinct categories than those used to assess normal communication development.

   1.   To Make Requests to Satisfy Needs and Wants, Seen and Unseen   Often children with moderate to severe handicaps can make requests to satisfy a variety of visible needs and wants by any number of behaviors such as pointing, reaching, making noises, or verbally asking. However, some of the same children who readily request things seen, cannot ask for things that are not visible. Since many of the things that a child will need are not in his or her immediate environment, the need to distinguish between the two categories of requesting behaviors for obtaining things seen and things unseen can become an important variable in educational planning.

   2.   To Request Help   Requesting help is an extension of the previous function. Asking for help is another frequently employed form for making requests to satisfy needs and wants. It has been identified and separated from the general category of requesting behaviors because many children with moderate to severe handicaps, especially children with autism, will frequently request *things* they want, but rarely request help from another person. Many times adults are used as objects for retrieving the items needed. Adults are rarely considered partners in any problem solving situation. In order to plan effective communication programs, it is important to distinguish between making requests to satisfy needs and wants and the special case of asking for help.

3. *To Protest*   Protesting has been left as it is in normal communication development. Protesting includes all behaviors a child may use in order to say "No" to activities, toys, food, or tasks.

4. *To Respond to a Social Initiative*   The function of responding to a social initiative and the next two functions listed are variations of the ability to engage in some form of social contact. All of the following functions require some sense of social behavior on the part of the child to successfully utilize these communicative functions. The functions listed above (requests to satisfy needs, requesting help, and protest) do not require any social skills, that is, they do not demand any sustained interaction with another person. Other people, in fact, are only agents through which those functions are fulfilled. Of the functions requiring social skillfulness, responding to a social initiative probably requires the least. If a child reacts to any social contact from another, this function can be met. The reaction can be as sophisticated as responding verbally to initiated conversation or it can be as simple as a child allowing himself or herself to be led to an activity by another person.

5. *To Initiate Social Interaction*   Initiating social interaction requires much more sophistication in social skills. In order to initiate social interactions, a child must take the initiative and seek out another individual. This can be done verbally by asking questions or making a statement directly to another person. A nonverbal initiation might be made by climbing into someone's lap, touching a person's face, or taking another by the hand and leading him or her somewhere.

6. *To Maintain Social Interaction*   To maintain social interaction, a child must possess as much or more social awareness as in the previous function. This ability can exist in a child who is nonverbal or preverbal as well as a child who is verbal. Obviously, being able to carry on a conversation, even a very simple one, is maintaining social contact. As long as the child responds in an appropriate manner, even if only in simple three-word sentences, phrases, or single words, the social interaction is being maintained. Similarly, a child who is nonverbal or preverbal can maintain social contact. This might be accomplished by turning pages in a book the child has brought you to read, or bringing you more books or objects to play with, or even just smiling or laughing when tickled and then poking out his or her stomach for more.

7. *To Ask for Reward or Affection*   Being able to ask for reward or affection is missing most often in children with autism. Unlike other children with moderate to severe handicaps, most autistic children do not seek out approval or positive physical contact from other people. For one reason or another, they do not seem to require these typically sought out qualities in human relationships. A child who is verbal would demonstrate this function by telling you about an accomplishment or asking for a hug. A child who is nonverbal or preverbal might seek reward by showing you something he or she has accomplished or may climb into your lap in order to receive affection.

8. *To Seek Comfort*   The child needing the ability to seek comfort seems to be more of a concern for teachers of children with autism. Because most children with autism do not relate to other people in a social context, it is not often that they will seek out another person when hurt or distressed. Most often you have to guess what is bothering the child. Typically, children with autism do not have normal response patterns to pain or distress. They often do not perceive fearful experiences as another person might. Some children with autism might show you where they are hurt. Others do not even seem to notice that they have been injured. A child who is verbal might tell you about pain or distress, but might be referring to an injury received in the past or an event that was described to him or her. Children who are nonverbal or preverbal may cry or whine when hurt, but rarely will they approach another person for comfort.

9.   *To Express an Interest in the Environment* Expressing an interest in the environment remains the same as described in the communication functions of normal development. Expressing an interest in the environment can be observed in a child who asks questions about his or her surroundings or just points to or holds up an object to another person.

10.   *To Communicate Experiences Not Shared by Others* Communicating experiences not shared by others also remains the same as described in the communication functions of normal development. The ability to communicate such experiences does depend, however, on the child having a considerable amount of some form of language. It also requires an ability to retain information and recall it within an appropriate context as well as an awareness of a listener's ability to understand. Most children with severe handicaps never demonstrate this level of sophistication in their communication.

11.   *To Play Act or Pretend* Play acting or pretending serves the same purpose as that described in normal development. For many children with severe handicaps it is a difficult function to assess. This function requires imagination. In children with autism, even those who are verbal often do not have the ability to retain information, rearrange it in a novel fashion, or create new, never experienced situations. It may be that the lack of imaginative play is a distinguishing characteristic between children with autism and other children (Wing, 1981).

Underlying any communication are the intentions (functions) of the speaker, which are listed in the two sections above. Regardless of whether or not verbal communication is used, communicative competence can be achieved if the child can influence the attitudes, beliefs, or behavior of the listener. The more language functions the child has and the more forms that he or she can utilize in communication, the greater his or her influence over the environment. This ability to express specific intentions should be the major focus of communication training programs aimed at increasing children's ability to operate in their environment. Knowing when and where to communicate and what cues/gestures to use when conveying an intended message is essential for building adequate communicative skills.

THE FORM OF COMMUNICATION

While the intent to influence the listener's attitudes, beliefs, or behavior is considered the function of language, the behavior used to convey the intended message is considered the communicative form. Intent can be conveyed to the listener using any form of communication that the listener understands. For example, a child may reliably communicate the desire to go outside by pulling an adult to the door and placing his or her hand on the doorknob. Even though this type of form is less sophisticated than talking, it serves its communicative function.

Communication takes many forms (e.g., talking, pointing to pictures, signing, gesturing). During early development, gesture and vocalization are frequently used to communicate. Even before the child learns to speak, these early forms are effective at fulfilling basic communicative functions. As children develop verbal language skills, they use an increasingly sophisticated language system to fulfill more functions. This is a complex system of symbolic representations (e.g., using words to represent objects, people, and/or events) and rules (i.e., grammar, sentence structure, word order) that govern interactions and are understood by both the speaker and the listener (Sailor et al., 1980). Learning such a sophisticated language system allows the child to reliably convey a number of messages to a variety of people, thereby effectively increasing control of the environment through communication and interaction.

A variety of forms can be used to produce the same result. Taking an adult to the bathroom, saying "Potty," and stating, "I have to use the bathroom," can all be considered different forms of the same communicative function. Even though each example varies in complexity, they all communicate the same intent, namely the need to go to the bathroom. Therefore, each of the above forms serves a single communicative function. Similarly, waving "hi" and saying "Nice to see you again," both serve as social greetings. Although the forms are quite different, each of them successfully conveys the intent of the speaker to the listener.

Children who are preverbal frequently use communication forms that are more difficult to understand than verbal communication. Pointing, gesturing, head movements, and vocalizations fall into this category. Before a child learns to say he or she does not like squash, the child effectively gets the message across by clenching teeth and turning his or her head away. Similarly, before a child can label "cracker" he or she can make a request by pulling you to a cupboard and reaching toward the appropriate box. Even though these communicative behaviors are less sophisticated than verbal communication, they are frequently used by children who are preverbal to express specific intent. When children use gestures to communicate, they rely on relevant parts of the context to convey their intent. The use of these contextual cues facilitates the listener's understanding of the message. The ability to effectively use context becomes a significant skill of early communicators. Without the ability to successfully use context, attempts to communicate may be misunderstood or misinterpreted. This leaves the speaker as well as the listener frustrated.

The contextual cues surrounding a single communication may include the setting, objects, and people within the setting, and the time of day and the event(s) that preceded the communication. In the example of the child requesting a cracker, he or she was able to use the setting (kitchen cupboard), parent (to reach the cracker), and relevant objects (cracker box) to obtain the cracker. If the child had not used each of these elements of the context, the communication would have been much less efficient and possibly misinterpreted.

EVALUATING CURRENT FORMS AND FUNCTIONS

An evaluation of each child's current ability to use communication forms to produce changes or affect the behavior of others (functions) is the first step toward developing an individualized comprehensive communication skill training program. Relevant features of communication patterns that need to be evaluated are:

1. The number of intentions (functions) a child can convey using any form
2. The quantity and quality of the communication form(s) used to convey the above intentions

3. The child's generalized ability to demonstrate functions using current forms (i.e.,
   those functions and forms that are appropriate in a variety of settings or situations with a variety of people)

Communication Form—Quantity and Quality

When developing a functional communication program, the communicative intentions must be considered first. The more intentions children can effectively convey to
listeners, the more influence they can exert over their environments. Increased ability
to express communicative intent provides maximum potential for social interaction.
Teachers must consider how often children who are verbal and nonverbal express a
particular intent; how many different intents are expressed; and whether each intent
generalizes to different listeners, situations, and settings.

For a communication form to operate effectively, it must convey an intended message and influence the behavior of others. In evaluating the communication abilities
of children who are verbal and nonverbal, it is important to identify all consistent
forms that a child uses in the environment to meet any of the communication functions. The forms may include talking, signing, gesturing, using symbols, or less conventional communicative behaviors, such as crying and tantrums. Children may use a
single form to meet a variety of functions or different forms for each separate function.
Using a single form to meet a variety of functions is exemplified by a child who points
to request an object, points to go outside, and points to himself or herself to gain
recognition. Similarly, children with limited communicative repertoires who cry until
fed, cry to gain attention, and cry until left alone, use a single form across several
functions. In both of these examples, the communicative form (pointing or crying) is a
single form that is used to meet a variety of communication functions. Using different
forms for different functions is exemplified by children who change their form depending on what they are trying to communicate. For example, a child who is preverbal or
nonverbal may point to request something, pull a parent to the door to go outside, lift
his or her arms to be picked up, and cry to gain attention. In this example, the child is
able to use a variety of gestures to convey numerous intentions (functions). As the
function changes, so does the form.

Each communication from can be evaluated in terms of the effect produced in
the environment, frequency of its expression, and the generalized ability to satisfy
each function across settings, people, and situations. Once these skills have been
evaluated, intervention efforts can focus on teaching acceptable forms to convey a
variety of intentions, thus increasing the potential for environmental influence and
social interaction.

Both conventional and nonconventional (idiosyncratic) communication forms
should be considered when evaluating a child's overall ability to communicate. Children who are language delayed often develop idiosyncratic communication patterns
that may not resemble formal language systems, but are effective at producing change
or increasing influence in the environment. These less conventional patterns may be
variations of preverbal forms used by nonhandicapped children, like gesturing, or may
be aberrant behavior such as tantrums or biting that the child has learned to use
communicatively. Some children have learned to communicate through extreme
forms of self-injurious behaviors (Carr & Durand, 1985; La Vigna & Donnellan, 1986). It
is important to remember that *any* form that conveys an intended message clearly
enough to obtain the desired response is effective and therefore an adequate form of
communication from the perspective of the "speaker."

Evaluating Form and Function Use in Children Who Are Nonverbal

Evaluating communicative abilities of children with moderate to severe handicaps is a difficult task. First you need to be able to determine which communicative functions the child has regardless of the quality of the form used. Then you need to turn your attention to the quality of the form as an effective mode of communication. In children who are nonverbal and preverbal, the quality of each communicative form currently used can be evaluated by answering the following questions:

1. *How reliable is a particular form at producing changes in the environment?* Once communication forms have been identified, it is necessary to determine how well they work. Do they consistently serve to change the behavior of others in the child's environment? Are they reliable at producing change with different people, in a variety of situations and settings, across a wide array of activities? Forms that are reliable at producing change across environments have a higher probability of being reinforced and therefore maintained. The effectiveness of any communication form is measured by how well it produces change in the behaviors of the listener(s).

2. *How easily can current communication forms be interpreted by others in the environment and how universal are the forms?* The more clearly communication forms are understood, the more likely they are to be effective. Idiosyncratic forms are often interpreted correctly by caregivers and teachers who are familiar with the communication of their children. However, these forms are likely to be misunderstood by people who have limited experience with these children. In addition, it is likely that idiosyncratic forms may not be identified as communicative behaviors, and will either be ignored or, worse yet, punished. Those forms that are easily understood or interpreted are more effective at producing change in the environment.

Communication forms that closely resemble those used by nonhandicapped children, or are part of universally understood language systems, are more likely to be recognized as communicative behaviors. Therefore, they are more likely to be responded to by listeners in the natural environment. Universal communication forms refer to those systems that are used or understood by the majority. The less universal the form, the more limited the audience. Children who use symbols, such as Blissymbols, as a primary communication mode, are limited to communicating only with others who know the same system. This may severely limit a child's opportunity to interact with others. The more universal the form, the more effective it will be with a large number of people across a variety of situations. Thus, the child's interaction potential is increased when universal forms are used.

3. *How portable is the child's current communication system?* A communication system that is easy to transport has a higher probability of being used in a number of settings. Bulky communication systems such as communication boards or picture books may limit the number of settings where the child can use them. Systems that are difficult to transport are likely to be taken along only when convenient, thus denying the user access to his or her primary mode of interaction. The more portable and less intrusive a communication form is, the more efficient it will be across settings.

4. *How acceptable is the child's current form to others he or she frequently interacts with?* If a child's current communication form is unacceptable or objectionable to people with whom he or she has daily interaction, he or she will not have an opportunity to use it. Regardless of the number of intentions a child can convey, if the form is unacceptable to caregivers or parents, it has a high probability of being ignored, making any communicative attempt nonfunctional.

The answers to questions 1–4 above provide specific information regarding the quality of current communication forms used by children who are nonverbal or preverbal. This information is useful when determining a child's current ability to use communication in context, and provides a reference point from which teachers can develop an appropriate communication program that will be functional for each student who is nonverbal.

Evaluating Form and Function Use in Children Who Are Verbal

A similar process can be used to evaluate the quality of communication forms currently used by children who are verbal. Many children with moderate to severe handicaps who are verbal will be children with autism. For those children, language abilities often will not coincide with communicative abilities. A careful analysis of the child's functional level as well as the quality of the forms he or she uses is critical to planning an effective communication program. The following questions will help you adequately evaluate the quality of verbal skills used by children who are language delayed or who have language deficiencies:

1. *Are current functions and forms used in a generalized manner?* The end product of a successful program is the generalized use of communicative functions and forms. Once current communicative functions and forms are identified, it is necessary to determine how widely each is used. The spontaneous use of communication across settings, people, and events allows children with language deficiencies to be competent users of communication.

2. *Can the child supplement verbal communications with additional information?* Frequently, children who are misunderstood can adequately convey a message by supplying the listener with additional information. This added information can be verbal (e.g., restating or rephrasing what he or she is trying to say, inserting missing words) or nonverbal (e.g., gesturing). The ability to use an alternate form when having difficulty communicating verbally is a skill that increases the effectiveness of the verbal form without the child needing additional verbal skill. The use of gesture as a supplemental form may allow the child with limited verbal abilities to effectively communicate with others. If the child you are evaluating repeats the current form even when it is clear that it is not communicating, you need to note this fact when evaluating his or her language. Children with autism will often develop a series of highly sophisticated language phrases that they will use in a wide variety of situations. Many times these phrases will import little understanding to the listener. It is important to determine whether the speaker is participating in helping the listener to understand by adding additional information and changing forms when necessary. Without an awareness of how they are influencing the communication process, children with moderate to severe handicaps, especially those with autism, cannot develop effective communicative behaviors.

3. *How easily can the intended message be understood by others?* For verbal utterances to be understood, they must be clearly articulated words, phrases, or sentences. Children with poor articulation are likely to be misunderstood by the majority of people with whom they interact. Regardless of how accurate a message is, if it is misunderstood due to poor articulation, it will not function adequately. A statement that is hard to understand is difficult to respond to. However, it is important to emphasize that before you attempt to refine the child's form, you must be sure that the child's functions are

intact. If the child is verbal but uses only a few functions, then your focus should be on developing new functions first before attending to the form.

It is also important to consider the word choice and sentence structure used by children with language deficiencies. Often poor word choice and/or poor sentence structure will inhibit the listener's understanding of the intended message. Ineffective word choice includes the addition, deletion, or substitution of words that change the content of the utterance. Word choice must be relevant to the content and context of the message to be adequately understood. Sentence structure must also be appropriate to the content and context of an utterance. This includes using questions or statements when and where they should occur and using pronouns appropriately. The more accurate a message is, the more effective and efficient it will be.

Identifying Patterns of Form and Function Use

Evaluating a child's ability to use form and function provides information relevant to establishing instructional targets. Before writing specific programs, you must identify the child's current ability to use communicative functions and determine the forms used to express those functions. The development of a longitudinal, comprehensive plan for remediation of communication deficiencies should include long-term goals for changes in both quality and quantity. Once these goals have been identified, short term objectives and specific educational targets can be selected.

Following the initial evaluation (taken from the section on Communication in Part 2 of each inventory) it is necessary to identify the pattern of form and function use exhibited by each student. Identifying communicative categories, or patterns of form and function, provides teachers with the information necessary to develop a longitudinal plan. The patterns of form and function indicated below may emerge when assessing a child's use of communication in context. The categories are not all-inclusive patterns. They do, however, provide a framework that can be used later for developing long-term educational goals, objectives, and instructional targets. Children with moderate to severe disabilities frequently display one of the following patterns of form and function use:

1. Adequate forms, multiple functions
2. Adequate forms, limited functions
3. Limited forms (including idiosyncratic or inappropriate forms), multiple functions
4. Limited forms (including idiosyncratic or inappropriate forms), limited functions
5. No identifiable forms or functions

The above patterns of form and function use cover a wide range of complexity and sophistication. IMPACT's communication training process is designed to first provide training in additional functions, if needed, and then provide training in forms. It is critical, however, that when you either shape new forms or refine current ones, you always keep the function intact. If the function is lost, through either inappropriate content or inappropriate context while training the child in the form, then instruction is pointless. You then have a child with language, but no ability to communicate.

When a child has a function deficiency (patterns 2, 4, and 5), training should focus on increasing the number of functions using whatever form the child currently has. When the child uses multiple functions (patterns 1 and 3), then instruction should focus on refining the form(s). If the child's only form is inappropriate (e.g., tantrums), then it may be necessary to shape that form into something more acceptable, like gesturing, while providing training in additional functions. In that case, training is provided in both form and function simultaneously within the context of naturally occurring routines to ensure improved communicative control across environments. Training autistic children in a form without regard to its function denies them the opportunity to experience the control and power that communicating encompasses.

Functional communication should be a major focus of instruction. Children with moderate to severe handicaps can be taught to participate in society if they learn to communicate effectively. To a great extent, their ability to participate in environments depends on their ability to communicate. Social interaction and general discourse are two abilities that define human existence. It is our ability to increase these capabilities in children with moderate to severe handicaps that determines a successful educational program. Part 3 of this handbook, "Learning with IMPACT," includes Chapter 10, "Teaching Communication in Context," which deals with teaching communication skills within routines. Each category of communication performance is discussed there in detail, including a description of deficiencies typically associated with each pattern, and strategies for remediating each deficiency.

Now you are ready to begin putting IMPACT into practice. Part 2 of this handbook, "Getting Started," will help you develop an implementation plan for your classroom and give you an overview of the instructional steps included in the curriculum. After you have mastered "Getting Started," you will have an overall design for your program, samples of forms and questions to go over with parents prior to enrollment of their child in your class, and a comprehensive outline of the instructional process.

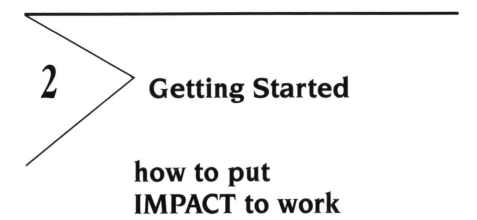

2 Getting Started

how to put IMPACT to work

6 How to Use IMPACT Inventories

The IMPACT curriculum has two similar inventories that are used to help teachers and parents set curriculum priorities. The IMPACT Environmental Inventory for the Home and Community (Home Inventory, see Appendix B) is used to obtain information about the student and his or her family. Part 1 covers the makeup of the family including the number of brothers and sisters. The family's favorite haunts and usual activities are sampled next. The communication patterns of the student, and how he or she communicates, are carefully documented in Part 2 of the survey. Part 3 samples the student's response to change, what he or she does with leisure time, and self-help skills that the student has mastered.

The IMPACT Environmental Inventory for School and Community (School Inventory, Appendix C) describes typical school and community activities, communication patterns at school, and the level of functional activities the student has access to. It parallels the Home Inventory. There are some additional questions that help document how your student functions in the school setting.

These inventories form the foundation of the IMPACT curriculum. They are your major assessment tools. Each inventory is broken down into three parts. You may want to use each part on a separate day. This will enable you to maximize the chances of getting the best responses to each question. Since IMPACT is a functional curriculum, it is essential that an accurate picture of how the child performs in various settings be available for program planning. It is also important that the number and types of environments frequented by the student be carefully described. These inventories provide this information. In addition to the samples that appear in Appendices B and C, the inventories are also available as individual booklets. (For ordering information, contact: Brookes Publishing Co., P.O. Box 10624, Baltimore, Maryland 21285-0624. Parent Guides are also available, packaged with Home and School Inventories.)

This chapter gives you information regarding the administration of the inventories, a step-by-step process for summarizing the information found in the two inventories, and a set of examples showing how you can translate this information into setting priorities and writing your individualized education program (IEP).

ASSESSING ENVIRONMENTAL NEEDS

In order for children with autism and other handicaps, moderate to severe, to effectively operate in a variety of home, school, and community settings, they must learn to respond to the requirements of each environment. Each setting requires that a variety of skills be performed with a certain amount of independence. While some skills are necessary in many settings (e.g., social and communication behaviors, mobility, and toileting), others are specific to a particular setting (e.g., doing the laundry or brushing teeth). When planning an educational curriculum that will ultimately lead to increased participation in these settings, both specific and general environmental requirements must be considered. A child who learns a few skills that apply to a limited number of settings will either have restricted access to a large number of activities and opportunities or be denied access altogether. In contrast, children who are taught to perform a wide range of skills across various environments, both current and future, will have an opportunity to participate more fully in society.

A functional curriculum aimed at teaching communication/social skills in a variety of settings must address not only the necessary skills a child needs for independent functioning in each setting, but also the context and cues associated with the use of each skill. Any communication skill taught without regard to its context is meaningless. Unless a skill can be successfully demonstrated in context, it is not functional. It is insufficient for children to learn to use isolated skills when presented with a standard set of cues, repeatedly, in the same instructional format. The important educational aim is for children with moderate to severe handicaps to learn to use appropriate skills when presented with the natural cues and consequences that occur in the environment. The IMPACT inventories provide the framework for assessing the level(s) of performance of your student at various tasks within several environments.

In laying the groundwork for a functional curriculum you will have to elicit the cooperation and support of the parents of your student to get the most complete information from the inventories. To do this you will need to spend some time providing parents with information about your program and how it will benefit their child. Three main themes need to be communicated before the inventories are given to the parents. First, each parent needs to have an understanding of functional curricula. This should include a thorough explanation of the rationale for its use, a discussion of expected outcomes for their child, and a description of what the educational process will look like. The parents will also need to know how functional curricula differ from other types of school programs. Many parents will have had some experience with other types of programs, and they will need to be given enough information for them to feel comfortable with the new curricula. It is important that an informed consensus be established during this process. Far too often, insufficient time is spent explaining to parents what is happening with their child's program and why. This investment in time at the beginning of the process will pay valuable dividends throughout the year.

The second main idea that needs to be explained to parents is what their role is in the educational process. In the IMPACT curriculum, parents are major providers of the information critical to developing programming. Functional curricula depend on teaching routines that will enable each child to have access to activities, events, or rewards that are valuable to him or her. Parents provide essential information about what a child likes, how he or she interacts in typical situations, and what activities and environments are available for training. Parents can also describe the idiosyncratic behaviors unique to their own child and can often give clues as to the functional intents of many of those behaviors. Without this information, you will not be able to adequately prepare a functional program for your student.

Third, you will need to communicate the role of the inventory. For many parents, the role of providing detailed assessment information will be new. In many school situations, this information is collected by professionals through formal assessment techniques. Parents are used to going to multidisciplinary team meetings and being told the "important" facts about their child. In the IMPACT program, parents provide a large portion of important information. Once parents understand the importance of what they are providing, they will usually complete the inventories with great care. Additionally, they will develop a feeling of cooperation and teamwork that will enable you to provide a more effective educational program for your student.

For many teachers, laying the groundwork for the inventories will require reorganizing their methods of working. For some, it may even require learning new skills. Even though the inventories take a substantial amount of time in an already busy schedule, it cannot be overemphasized how important the information contained in the inventories is to programming efforts. Equally important is the relationship that is formed between home and school during the inventory process. Although taking part in cooperative information gathering between teacher and parents may be a new role for both, it is a major vehicle for integrating home, community, and school environments into a comprehensive school program.

PARENTAL INVOLVEMENT

When approaching parents about their involvement in curriculum development, be sure they understand how important they are to the process of their child's program. The following seven points of the IMPACT curriculum are included here to help you organize your presentation. Special emphasis should be placed on how each point affects the parents and their child's program. To further aid parents in understanding the IMPACT curriculum process, you may refer to A *Parent Guide to Understanding the* IMPACT *Curriculum* in Appendix D.

1. *Parents possess critical knowledge of current home and community requirements.* Parents' knowledge of the child's current environments and of the skills that are necessary to function in them are the major source of information for determining curricular goals. Since parents live with the child and are often the ones who accompany the child in the community, they possess the best knowledge about skills that are now, or could potentially be functional. If the purpose of instruction is to prepare children to function as independently as possible once they leave school (not just instructing them to be good students), then instruction should improve the child's independent functioning in all environments. Parents are a major source of the information required to adequately program routines in environments outside the school.

2. *Instruction takes place in several environments.* The IMPACT curriculum is not only a school program. It involves simultaneous instruction in the home, school, and community. Functional skills must be taught in the context where they would normally occur. Instructional trials will occur at times when they would naturally occur throughout the day. Since children with autism and other moderate to severe handicaps have great difficulty generalizing skills, teaching in context, though sometimes more difficult, is a very efficient use of instructional time. By programming instructional activities so that they occur at the normal time and in the right place, the teacher can

make sure that the child not only learns the correct skill sequences, but also the right time and place to use them. Embedding instruction into natural routines cannot be overemphasized. It is the cornerstone of the IMPACT process.

3.   *Parents are involved on an ongoing basis.* The amount and types of parent input and continuing involvement in the IMPACT curriculum are different from that in most other curricula. Active parent participation is a necessary and integral part of the process. The parents will be needed to: 1) provide information about the child's needs and abilities, 2) work with the teacher in developing home and community program targets, and 3) provide information regarding the effectiveness of the instruction by conducting generalization probes in the home and community. Parents will be involved in planning and evaluation throughout the school year, with their involvement going beyond the IEP process. Some extra effort, of course, will have to be expended in forming and maintaining these new relationships with parents. The end product, however, is well worth the effort.

4.   IMPACT *includes a process for determining the individual educational needs of each student;* new skills are taught in adaptable classrooms and possibly other settings. Needs are identified by parents and teachers and are selected according to the skill requirements of the child's home, school, and community environments. Because these settings are so variable across children, the curriculum results in many different classroom activities occurring simultaneously. To ensure the functionality and transferrence to the natural environment of each child's program, instruction may take place in settings outside of the classroom. Functional routines carried out within the classroom will be more mobile than those in traditional programs, as children move around engaged in purposeful activities. Because these routines will be longer than those in traditional programs, fewer of them will be scheduled in a day. There will be fewer IEP goals, and they will be more integrated than usual. (See Chapter 8, "Writing the Individualized Education Program" for further discussion.) The notion of curricular areas (e.g., language, fine motor, cognitive) will give way to more functional IEP goals (e.g., independent community mobility, grocery shopping, requesting help).

The appearance of the classroom will change. Students will not be sitting at their desks for instruction on isolated skills. Instead, teaching will consist of instructional routines. Whole skill sequences will be taught at their appropriate time and have purposeful outcomes. How different classrooms will look will depend on what type of programming was previously used, the functioning level of the children in the classroom, and the particular priorities targeted for children in the classroom. In most cases the observable differences in the classroom will be substantial.

5.   *Some risks are involved.* We believe, of course, that the IMPACT curriculum provides a good, longitudinal program for children with moderate to severe handicaps, including autism. As usual, however, there are potential risks of which parents should be made aware. During the transition from one curriculum to another, as with any change in routine, there may be some disruption in the classroom. There may even be some apparent deterioration in performance. Some children may revert to less desirable behaviors to try to regain the structure(s) they had in the past. Such problems could be due to the change alone, or they could be due to switching from contrived cues and artificial rewards to a more naturally occurring set of cues and consequences. The problems should be temporary, however, and they are usually alleviated when the children (and teacher) adjust to the change.

One other potential risk is that the child's subsequent school placement may use nonfunctional curricula. Parents should be aware that future placements that use functional curricula may not be developed (depending on the resources of your district). With your help, they should begin to request that schools develop functional curricula at all levels. Even though longitudinal functional curricula may not exist at present, this should not detract from the child learning functional skills now.

6. *Other professionals who interact with their child (e.g., communication disorders specialists, occupational therapists, bus drivers) play an important role.* The major role of all staff interacting with a child in the IMPACT project is to facilitate the acquisition of functional skills in *naturally occurring contexts.* An occupational therapist may still set fine and gross motor goals for a child, but these goals will be met through instruction within routines. Communication disorders specialists will not just provide instruction in the how of communication, but also the where and when. In fact, the role of all those working with the child will be to aid him or her in learning the how, where, and when of various skills.

7. *How the program works must be explained.* Each step of the IMPACT curriculum should be carefully explained to the parents. This will prevent misunderstanding later. A truly functional educational program must encompass all environments in which the child participates. The enhancement of independent functioning within those settings will increase the likelihood of the child participating in the least restrictive environments possible. With parents and teachers working together, each child's potential for independent functioning can be enhanced.

To assist you in your discussion with parents, use the sample Parent Interview Form shown on page 40. In addition to listing each of the areas that should be covered, space is provided so that you may note any parental concerns or other responses.

HOW TO ADMINISTER THE HOME INVENTORY

At first glance, the Home Inventory looks quite intimidating. Any time you ask parents to fill out a lengthy form, there is going to be some resistance. It will be necessary to anticipate these problems and help the parents understand the purpose of the inventory before you give it to them. A section on what the inventories do is included in the Parent Guide (Appendix D) for you to use when approaching parents about IMPACT. It is designed to help parents understand the need for functional curricula and appreciate the importance of the Home Inventory. It also answers some of the most frequently asked questions.

Since each school district is different, you may want to adapt this Parent Guide to your own particular situation. For example, if you are beginning a new functional curriculum program in your school, you may want to add more information regarding functional curricula and how they are different from school programs for children who are nonhandicapped, which are more familiar to the parents. Blank pages at the end of the Parent Guide booklets provide space for some of the adaptations you may wish to make.

If, on the other hand, you are modifying an existing program, you might want to emphasize similarities and differences between the two programs, and focus more on how the new curriculum will increase the independent functioning of each child. Here you would want to include in the Parent Guide those parts of the introduction to this handbook that explain how a functional curriculum differs from other curricula for children with moderate to severe handicaps.

In either case, it is important that you use the inventory in such a way that it

IMPACT PARENT INTERVIEW FORM

Curricular components	Parents' concerns and comments
Inventories	
Instructional environments	
Parent involvement	
Function/form	
Communication functions	
Routines	
How classroom will change	
Role of other professionals	
Risks	
Generalization probes	

produces the most accurate picture of how your student functions in several environments. This often takes some time at the beginning of each program, but when you begin planning your program you will find it was time well spent.

There are several methods for actually administering the inventory. Which method, or combination of methods, you use will depend on many factors. If the parents are fairly sophisticated and experienced in planning priorities and providing information in written form, then you might want to either send the inventory to them with a cover letter, or drop it by their home. (An example of a cover letter is provided with the inventory in Appendix A.) You could also send them a copy of the Parent Guide (Appendix D) to help them understand how a functional curriculum works and how important the inventory is to their child's program. Or, you might want to send them Part I only and then wait until they return it before sending the next part. This way you could judge whether or not you had explained the program carefully enough the first time.

If, on the other hand, you have parents who are less sophisticated or experienced with functional curricula, you might want to set up an appointment to interview them using the inventory as a guide for your questions. These interviews can be either in person or over the telephone. If you interview in person, you will also probably want to take a copy of the Parent Guide and a blank inventory to leave with them after you have gone. This will enable them to read about the program and help them remember other things that they might have forgotten the first time the program was explained to them.

Regardless of how you administer the inventory, you should always make a follow-up contact to spot check items on the inventory for accuracy and to clarify other items that were unclear. These second contacts will not only increase the accuracy of the information you gather, they will also enable you to reinforce the parents for the effort and time they spent filling out the forms. Many times, second contacts will provide an opportunity for a parent to express a special concern or enable him or her to ask you questions about the program. It is very important to provide these opportunities early on in the development of the program. Many potential problems in communication and understanding can be prevented if you take the time to follow-up after the inventory is completed.

HOW TO ADMINISTER THE SCHOOL INVENTORY

The School inventory provides information in three areas. First, it will enable you to assess the various activities of your student within the school setting. Second, it will enable you to compare your student's performance in school with that reported in the Home Inventory. Third, it will enable you to evaluate your current school program with regard to access to functional activities and natural environments.

Before you complete the inventory you will need to take time to get to know your children in various settings. It is important to feel comfortable with your understanding of how a child behaves before you complete the inventory. If you come to an item that you are unsure of, set up some time with the child to explore how he or she behaves in that circumstance.

After you have completed the inventory, be sure to check your perceptions. You might want to complete a second inventory and compare answers, or you can ask others who work with your student such as paraprofessionals, volunteers, communication disorder specialists, occupational therapists, or physical therapists to complete another inventory. Your goal is to make your inventory as reflective of typical performance as possible.

SUMMARIZING INVENTORY RESULTS

Before developing a comprehensive program to teach skills in context, the following questions must be answered by teachers and parents:

1. In what environments does the child currently participate? What other settings would the child be likely to have access to if he or she had the skills?
2. What are the communication and interaction skills needed to meet the demands of those different environments?
3. In each environment, what other skills are required that the child must learn to be successful? What is the child's current skill level in these environments?
4. What are the contextual cues that exist in each environment?
5. How can the teacher utilize natural situations to provide training in these skills in context?
6. What outcomes (critical effects) are there for the child in each environment?
7. What are the parents' priorities?

Once these questions have been answered, a comprehensive educational plan can be designed. The information needed to answer these questions can be found in the Home and School Environmental Inventories.

Both the Home and School Inventories are summarized on a series of summary sheets (which are included after their respective inventories in Appendices B and C). The four summary sheets for each inventory are briefly described below.

The IMPACT *environment summary* (home version, school and community version) is used to record the number and types of environments in which a student participates. It also records the level of supervision that is required in each setting for the student to operate effectively.

On the IMPACT *communication summary* (home version, school and community version) you will record each of the communicative functions that are reported on the inventories. The specific form(s) that each student uses to communicate his or her intent(s) are also noted on these forms. Finally, any person(s) who are the usual targets of a communicative act are noted here.

The IMPACT *preference summary* (home version, school and community version) lists activities, games, and toys that are preferred by your student. Places are provided for you to note the degree of supervision required for each item. If the games recorded have been adapted to meet special needs of your student, it should be noted on this form. Also, special people who can evoke exceptional performances from your student should be listed. Foods that your student likes and dislikes are recorded on page 2 of this summary. The final section gives you a place to note any idiosyncratic problems that need to be avoided until you can design effective alternatives for dealing with them.

Finally, the IMPACT *problems summary* (home version, school and community version) lists the various behavioral problems that the student presents. There is a place to note the setting, task, and/or command that surrounds the problem, and any particular person who is usually involved.

Once you have summarized the results of both inventories on the sheets provided, you are ready to begin setting priorities and developing the IEP. You should have a clear picture of how your student functions in a variety of different settings and situations. Of course, no single assessment is always 100% accurate. You will always want to check your perceptions to make sure that you are using the most up-to date and accurate information when planning programs.

After programs are designed and implemented, most changes will be based on the instructional data you collect. It is a good idea, however, to return to these inventories once a year to check the overall focus of your programming. Ask yourself whether your students are increasing their independent functioning in current environments outside the school setting, and whether the skills you are teaching are skills that will continue to be useful in years to come. You can use the inventories to help you retain the complete picture of what you are trying to accomplish for each student.

Another use of the inventories and inventory summary sheets is to communicate progress to the parents. Often the data we collect are too technical for most parents to interpret. The inventories and summary sheets can show growth in several ways. You can document increases in environments participated in, functions used, and activities preferred by each student. You can also show the decrease in supervision required and the lessening of problem situations that remain for each student. Therefore, the inventories are an essential part of the initial planning process and are useful tools for continued planning and communication of progress throughout the student's school years.

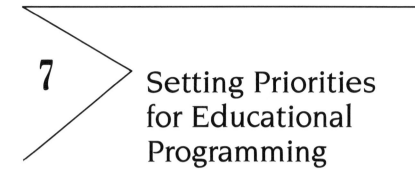

7 Setting Priorities for Educational Programming

After the Home and School Inventories have been completed, the teacher should select tentative priorities for educational programming and transfer them to the IMPACT Priority Summary Sheet, on which two areas of priority are noted. First, the Overall Short-Term Priorities are tabulated from the two inventories. Comparisons are made between home and school priorities. Agreements are noted in the center column as these will become major goals for all concerned. Differences in priorities will occur in most cases. These differences will be discussed in the multidisciplinary team meetings, and the team will try to reach consensus as to which goals should be addressed first. This is also a good time to clarify any areas of confusion that might have arisen during the inventory process. The resolution of differences should be easier for everyone because the inventory process develops a professional relationship between parents and teachers from the start.

The IMPACT Priority Summary Sheet also includes a space for critical priorities. Critical priorities are reserved for major problem areas that require immediate attention. For example, if a child is running away and endangering himself or herself, planning an effective alternative will be a critical priority. Other critical priorities include behaviors that endanger other children, or behaviors that prevent the child from being allowed to remain in a school or home environment. These problem areas must be addressed immediately.

After the teacher has analyzed the two inventories, and listed the short-term and critical priorities, the IEP Tentative Goal List can be completed. After these goals are discussed by all the members of the multidisciplinary team, they will become the major instructional goals for the year. Whenever team members set priorities, they will always have some differences. Every skill needed in every area of functioning cannot be taught at the same time. Some decisions will have to be made regarding which skills should be taught first. Here are three criteria to consider when determining priority goals: 1) selecting priorities that can be used in multiple environments over those that can be used in only one environment, 2) selecting priorities that are longi-

IMPACT PRIORITY SUMMARY SHEET

Overall Short-Term Priority List

Parent(s)	Agr.[1]	Teacher(s)

Critical Priority List

Parent(s)	Agr.	Teacher(s)

IEP Tentative Goal List

[1]Agr. = agreement. Check this column when parents and teachers agree on priority.

tudinal, that is, those with both current and future use, and 3) selecting priorities that are age-appropriate. Each of these critieria is discussed below.

Select priorities that can be used in multiple environments over those that can be used in only one environment. When selecting priorities, be sure to pick those that can be used in multiple settings. Targeting skills that are frequently required in as many of a child's environments as possible will increase the child's ability to handle environmental demands, thereby helping to maximize his or her participation. For example, a child who is not toilet trained and needs assistance numerous times a day in a variety of settings will require a great deal of supervision. Acquisition of skills that enable the child to handle toileting without assistance will enhance the child's independent functioning in a variety of settings.

Select priorities that are longitudinal. If we keep in mind that the goal of education is to prepare children to function as independently as possible in adulthood, it is difficult to justify the instruction of skills that will not be useful in the child's future. Many children have spent countless instructional sessions learning "puts together three-piece puzzle"—a recreational/leisure skill that will stigmatize anyone over 3 years old. When selecting priorities, then, remember to ask not only whether the skill is functional for the child now, but whether it will serve a purpose for the child in the future. Techniques should be used that will integrate the fine motor and cognitive skills involved in learning how to assemble a puzzle into a more longitudinal goal.

Select age-appropriate priorities. When prioritizing goals, you should also consider the age of the child and what other children his or her age do. Four-year-old children usually do not do the laundry, just as 10-year-old children do not ride tricycles. More age-appropriate goals might be dressing routines for a 4-year-old or riding a bicycle for a 10-year-old. Selecting goals that are age-appropriate for your students will provide the opportunity for them to learn functional behaviors that are socially appropriate. In many cases, you will want to plan ahead and provide training in skills that will help students have access to future environments. Those skills will enable them to perform successfully in environments targeted for access in a couple of years and will likely be skills that require a substantial amount of instruction for the children to reach proficiency. For example, a 10-year-old who will have access to a baseball team when he or she enters junior high school at 12 years of age could begin acquiring the skills of the game now. If it is appropriate for a 16-year-old to play video games and the child is now 13, you may want to begin instruction now because acquisition rates frequently are slow. This may increase the possibility of interaction with peers now and at a later date. Remember, though, that each skill taught must also allow the student to achieve some current critical effect. Be sure to design instructional programs that achieve immediate benefits along with the promise of a long-term reward.

At first glance, longitudinal and age-appropriate goals may appear to compete. This need not be the case. For example, when you teach a child to operate a record player, the type of player (Fisher-Price to Pioneer) and the level of music (Cinderella to Beethoven) can change as the child gets older. Over time, however, the skill of playing records stays the same. Whenever possible, select goals that are both age-appropriate and longitudinal.

SELECTING SPECIFIC IEP GOALS

It is important to remember that the parents need to be an integral part of each step in the development of their child's IEP. Parental involvement increases the likelihood that parents will become active partners in designing and implementing programs at home, in the school, and in the community. Involving parents will help ensure that the child's program is functional and that it really addresses the needs of the child in his or her current environments. For example, any crisis situation at home that is identified through the the environmental inventories should be selected as a priority. A crisis situation might include aggressive or unmanageable behavior in public that forces a parent to remain at home with the child. Within a functional curriculum, programming routines to address needs at home and school become inseparable. A crisis at home can result in the child being removed from the home and subsequently from public school placements. If a crisis situation at home leads to the child's removal from your classroom, any other educational programming that you have planned becomes meaningless.

The following is a list of points for you to consider when reviewing the summary of educational priorities for your student and planning his or her IEP:

1.   Compare home and school priorities. If there are general skills (e.g., requesting help, following directions, playing alone, toileting, dressing, mobility) that the child does not complete with an acceptable amount of independence, target those skills first. This will decrease the child's need for supervision both at school and at home.

2.   Identify any discrepancies between the child's performance at home and at school. Routinely, children's behavior reflects what is expected of them. If expectations are different across environments, the child will perform inconsistently. Eliminating discrepancies across environments can result in the child making consistent use of the skills he or she knows.

3.   Select for instruction the routines that require large amounts of assistance or supervision at the present time. Those should be routines that are a high priority for the parents and are functional both in current and future environments.

4.   Select additional routines for instruction that the child can almost perform independently. With minimal instruction, the child can learn to perform these whole routines independently, thus increasing his or her ability to function effectively and with less supervision.

There may be other guidelines you prefer to follow when selecting instructional targets for inclusion on IEPs. Regardless of the priority system you use, a comprehensive educational program should include instructional activities to address needs in each of the child's environments: home, school, and community.

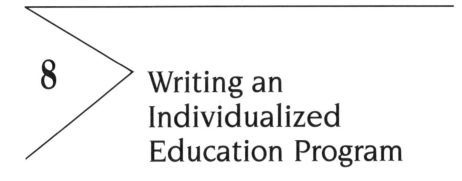

Writing an Individualized Education Program

Writing an individualized education program (IEP) is one of the most important parts of the instructional process. It becomes your road map for programming. A good IEP should reflect a careful analysis of the Home and School Inventories, clearly stated priorities, and specific information needed to plan an effective educational program. We cannot, of course, provide you with the exact form to use. Each school district has its own variation that reflects a district style and the state legal requirements. This chapter of the handbook is designed to help you create useful IEPs. It will explain what an instructional routine is, how to write an IEP that is functional, and how to select the instructional environments for your IEP. When you apply the information contained in this chapter, you should be able to define clearly the goals of instruction, and be ready to develop instructional plans.

INSTRUCTIONAL ROUTINES

Before you can write an effective IEP, you need to familiarize yourself with the notion of instructional routines. An instructional routine is a sequence of skills that produces a desired effect for the child in a natural context. Your instructional program will consist of a series of instructional routines. Each routine will begin with a natural cue that exists in the child's environment; the routine will end when the child has achieved the critical effect. Routines are designed to include all the steps necessary to achieve a critical effect. Communication skills are integrated into each routine so that language training will be in natural settings and in conditions that are similar to those required of your student each day. Instead of having programs that cover each of the basic developmental areas, your IEP will reflect a series of instructional routines that flow from one to the other. Each routine will lead to a critical effect and will reflect the needs listed on your Priority Summary Sheet.

A routine is similar to a traditional task analysis (see Chapter 9, page 71 for further discussion of task analyses). There are, however, several very important differences. First, a routine includes all the steps necessary to have access to a particular activity or event in the natural context. If a child wanted to get something to eat, and he or she were sitting in a chair in another room, an instructional routine would include all the steps required to get from the chair (natural cue: feeling hungry) to getting something to eat (critical effect: feeling full). These steps would include motor skills, cognitive skills, and communication skills integrated into an instructional sequence that produced the desired result for the child. By using routines as a method of instruction, the teacher can provide an instructional program that will be easily maintained and that will readily transfer to nonteaching settings.

A second difference between instructional routines and the more familiar task analyses may be found in the points at which instruction begins and ends. Instructional routines begin with the natural cue in the envrionment and end with the achievement of the critical effect. Looking at our Getting Something to Eat program again, the natural cue is feeling hungry (or communicating that feeling) and the critical effect is feeling full. In a more traditional task analysis, the last steps would be cleaning up (Van den Pol et al., 1981).

This leads us to the third major difference between a routine and many task analyses: the ending point of all routines is a critical effect *for the child*. Many instructional programs that are designed for children with moderate to severe handicaps have as their goal a critical effect for the teacher or parent. For an instructional routine to be effective, you will need to design programs so that they lead to critical effects for the student.

The differences between traditional task analyses and instructional routines are subtle, but very important. Understanding the subtle differences can often mean the difference between successful and unsuccessful instruction. A more detailed discussion of how routines have on impact on your teaching will be covered in more detail in Chapter 9, "The Instructional Process."

SELECTING SKILL AREAS

There are four general types of priority function areas that can be obtained from the inventories for use in writing IEPs: 1) communication/social, 2) transition, 3) recreation/leisure, and 4) self-help. Instruction in each function area produces specific skills for your student. If your student can learn the skills necessary to master each general function area, then he or she will have considerably more autonomy in a multitude of environments. When you review the list of goals on the Priority Summary Sheet, you will want to ensure that each of these general areas is addressed. Some goals may include more than one area. Others may address only one specific area. When you construct an IEP, program goals should be developed that integrate as many skills as possible into functional routines that will increase the independent functioning of the student.

1.   Communication/social skills are the most important any student can acquire. Communication/social functions increase the child's opportunities to participate in social interactions and give each student more influence in determining what happens to him or her. The student who can communicate effectively is more able to make

clear his or her needs, establish interactions with others, and ask for a variety of things that can only be obtained through communication.

2.   Common traits of children with moderate to severe handicaps, especially children with autism, are their insistence on sameness and ritualistic behaviors. For these children, transitions can be extremely difficult. They do not know how to move from one activity to another or when to end an activity. They may perseverate on a task without recognizing a beginning and end and often may tantrum if interrupted. Transition skills aid your student in adapting to changes in his or her environment and recognizing the beginning and end to a variety of activities or tasks. Most environments that your student will have access to are filled with daily changes and unpredictability. Having the skills necessary to make easy transitions will give the child more independent mobility and increase his or her abilities to participate in various environments.

3.   The function of recreation/leisure skills is to provide the child with a variety of free time activities. Many children with moderate to severe handicaps have never learned recreation skills (e.g., occupying spare time, interacting with others). Far too often they have not been taught the skills necessary to engage others in play nor have they learned to develop their own activities when others are not around. Since children with moderate to severe handicaps often acquire new skills at a very slow rate, you will need to select the recreation skills you teach very carefully. It will do your student little good to learn skills that are not age-appropriate. The skills you select should be longitudinal (useful throughout the student's life) and also immediately useful. If a child acquires recreation/leisure skills that are age-appropriate and immediately useful, participation in the environment is dramatically increased. This successful participation becomes the critical effect for the skill you select. Without this effect, teaching the new skill will be difficult and the results you achieve may be temporary.

4.   Personal independence in daily living is the function of self-help skills. The more skills your student can perform independently (e.g., dressing, mobility, meal preparation and clean up, toileting), the less dependent he or she is on others. Acquisition of these skills increases the likelihood of the child living as independently as possible. As independence increases, your student's ability to influence events around her or him also increases. It is this overall increase in influence and independence that defines the increasing quality-of-life for all children with moderate to severe handicaps.

SELECTING INSTRUCTIONAL SITUATIONS

Another component of writing the IEP is the selection of the instructional context in which you are going to teach. IMPACT has identified three general situations you might consider for teaching routines in context: 1) routines that have a natural context at school, 2) routines for which a functional context at school is created, and 3) routines that require having access to out-of-school (i.e., home and community) environments. IMPACT's philosophy is that children should receive instruction in context on skills that enable maximum participation in a wide variety of environments. Since a majority of the longitudinal, age appropriate activities occur outside the school setting, you should plan for out-of-school teaching. How much community based instruction is required will, of course, depend on each child's priorities.

Some skills may not necessarily require community access. A parent priority of toilet training, for example, requires cooperation between parents and teachers but does not necessarily initially require access to environments other than home and at school. In addition, dressing and undressing routines call for skills that are usually targeted for instruction at home and at school. There may be instances, however, where parents target routines that require instruction in the community. A parent may want a child to go to the store independently, eat appropriately at a restaurant, go visit a relative or friend, or even just use an unfamiliar bathroom. Situations like these will necessitate targeting other settings for instruction or at least for an assessment of generalization.

Routines with Natural Context at School

When each child's priorities for instruction have been decided, you may find that some will have a natural, functional context during the school day. To determine which priorities have this natural context, examine the routines that already exist in your classroom. Look at what is required of the child to move through the school day. Getting from the bus to the classroom, setting up and putting away materials, moving from one activity to the next, lunch, gym (including dressing and undressing), recess, and toileting are all examples of school routines. These routines will differ somewhat depending on the classroom and activities of a particular school. For example, swimming once a week might be a routine for one classroom and not another, as might music or going to the library.

For some younger children you may find that many instructional priorities have a context at school. Children who need a lot of assistance with basic routines (e.g., communication/social, mobility, toileting, and eating) may spend a good portion of their day learning these skills. Remember, though, that even skills that have a natural functional context at school should have multisetting and longitudinal use.

When the required activities for functioning in the school are identified, it may become apparent that they call for skills that are parts of routines in other environments. Toileting, for example, is a routine that is required not only in school, but in most other environments where more than a brief stay is necessary. Dressing and undressing skills are required both at home and in some recreational programs; eating occurs at home, school, and many community sites (e.g., restaurants, parks, neighbors' homes); and mobility skills are required across environments.

Though you may find a context at school for many routines, it is important to keep in mind the difficulty children with moderate to severe handicaps have in generalizing the use of skills. Training a child in only one or two environments (e.g., home and school) will greatly limit his or her ability to function in the community. So, even for younger children, always have routines that allow for some community access. This will give the child the opportunity to practice necessary skills in a variety of settings as well as to learn skills essential for community participation.

Routines for which Context Can Be Created

In addition to routines that are naturally occurring during the school day, there will be priority skills for which a functional context can be developed. Your strategy will be to change the school format to create a functional need for the target skill. If a priority for a child is to learn to eat family style (i.e., serving oneself, then passing the food to the next person), lunch and snack routines could be arranged so that priority is taught within a functional context. Dressing and undressing routines can also have a natural context within the school day if children must change clothes for swimming, gym, or perhaps even recess. Many of the necessary routines of the home can be worked into the teaching context of the school day. Toileting, dressing and undressing, brushing teeth, combing hair, setting and cleaning up the lunch table, independent and cooperative play, and social and communication instruction can all become natural events at school.

An example of a routine for which context was created at school is Preparing to Eat. This routine can include instruction on skills such as responding to the cue that it is time to eat, setting the table, finding the food, transporting it to the table, finding a place to sit, and practicing communication skills that are priorities for the child. The time associated with food consumption is a valuable instructional period, not only for perfecting eating skills, but for meeting social and communication targets. Restructuring the eating situation (e.g., having a child serve the food or having family style meals) can greatly facilitate interaction and communication. A couple of snacks during the day, in addition to lunch, can give the children more opportunities to practice these skills. The time spent in instruction of eating skills, including preparing to eat and cleaning up, becomes greatly expanded. As most children respond favorably to food, activities associated with it can provide a very reinforcing learning environment. Since most people eat out in the community, this could become a routine for every child to practice both in the classroom and in the community.

Additional practice on many community skills can be done without leaving the school grounds. For example, if a child needs to learn to accompany his or her parents on community errands, he or she must possess, at a minimum, the following behaviors: 1) coming when called, 2) sitting or standing for a specified period of time (the amount of time depending on the environment), and 3) staying near the parents when walking. Instruction in these skills can be provided throughout the day in the school building and on the school grounds. Training in independent mobility skills can also be provided at school by having a child run necessary errands.

Routines that are programmed by creating a context within the school day have several implications for managing resources. Since instructional programming is done within school boundaries, scheduling, money, and transportation for community access are required less often. The need for developing additional personnel or other resources is also minimized since most resources should already be within the school or easily added to the school routine.

Caution must be taken, however, to ensure that you are producing the desired effect in other environments. If instruction is only taking place in the school with school personnel, the child's learning may be environment or person specific. That is, the child may have problems generalizing the skills learned at school to other settings. Therefore, although the teacher/school will have the primary role for instructing the child, trying the skill in the natural environment is critical to ensure that generalization is taking place and the skills are truly functional for the child in other (i.e., out-of-school) settings.

Extra-School Instruction: When Context Cannot Be Created at School

It is not always possible to create a functional program in school for all skills targeted on the inventories. Going to a house of worship or a movie, shopping at grocery and department stores, and eating at restaurants do not have natural functional equivalents at school. When the context for instruction does not exist at school, you will need to create instructional programs in other environments where a functional context exists.

Obtaining access to other/future environments is a critical component of the IMPACT curriculum, though it may initially present some difficulties in implementation. Creativity and commitment on the part of the teacher are required. Strategies for managing resources (i.e., time, travel, money, personnel) need to be developed to obtain access to community environments. These programs will require additional people in certain cases. You will need to develop instructional programs that can be run by others. Before planning a schedule, you and the parents should agree on which environment(s) should be targeted for initial instruction. Each environment selected should not only require the use of the priority target skills but also be an environment that is visited frequently by the student outside the school day. If the family of your student never has access to the environments you are using for training (or environments similar to it), practice will be limited and generalization severely hampered.

You will also have to decide where and how often to participate in the environments that have been selected as instruction sites. Remember, when setting up the schedule, it is also a good idea to schedule some visits during which no instruction takes place. Observations of how well your student does without the structure that surrounds the instructional process will be measured instead. This will let you know how well your instruction is progressing, and it will also indicate what changes you might make in the program. More details regarding the use of generalization probes are included in Chapter 9, "The Instructional Process."

When developing your resources, look at all potential sources. Transportation could be provided by the school, public transportation, or teachers' and parents' cars. When planning personnel needs, if more than one classroom is involved in the curriculum, use a team teaching strategy—one teacher instructing in the school while the other is teaching in the community. Or cooperate with other classrooms, having them take children for a "mainstreamed" period (with certain children designated as special helpers) while you conduct the community-based programs. With a little reinforcement and training, community volunteers and other students at the school can also become valuable human resources for community access.

There may be some community access programs for which you are unable to provide sufficient instructional time in the natural environment (e.g., you or the parents are able to have access to the target setting only once per week). In cases like these, it is possible to provide additional practice of the skill by creating simulations in the classroom that approximate the functional context by employing rehearsal strategies (Freagon et al., 1981). Rehearsal strategies are designed to replicate for the student the sequence of activities that are found in the community setting. This involves doing a task analysis for the targeted site to determine the simulation of the physical layout and the sequence of the task analysis. Obviously, the task analysis should be as similar as possible to one that would be used if instructional sessions were taking place in the natural environment. In general, rehearsal strategies will encompass the following:

1. The materials required to simulate the natural environment
2. A sequence of activities for the group (if applicable), the teachers, and individual students
3. A procedure for simulating the activities at the training site

The major pitfall of this instructional strategy is that generalization problems may occur. Learning a series of skills in a simulated setting does not ensure that the child can successfully perform those skills in the natural environment. Therefore, this strategy should only be viewed as a means of giving the child additional practice on the routine skills. The routine must still be probed on a regular basis in the natural environment. Probes will provide information on what skills the child has acquired and which have failed to generalize; based on this information, changes can be made in the instruction to facilitate generalization. (For additional information regarding methods to promote generalization when classroom simulations are employed, see Horner, McDowell, & Bellamy [1986].)

WRITING YOUR GOALS AS FUNCTIONAL ROUTINES

Traditional IEPs consist of goals in various developmental areas. These goals are usually gross motor, fine motor, preacademic or cognitive, self-help, communication, and social. IMPACT goals, however, reflect the integrated functional routines that will be used by the child throughout his or her life. The following goals were taken from a series of traditional IEP goals for some actual students with moderate to severe handicaps:

1. Gross motor: Throw and catch an 8 inch rubber ball for 5 minutes.
2. Fine motor:
    a. Cut a circle, square, and triangle.
    b. Complete a three-piece wooden puzzle.
3. Cognitive/Preacademic:
    a. Discriminate 6 colors in a two-choice matching task.
    b. Write the letters of his or her name.
    c. Match 1:1 correspondence up to the number 5.
4. Self-help:
    a. Handle toileting independently.
    b. Dress independently.
    c. Identify articles of clothing.
5. Communication:
    a. Identify and name five objects.
    b. Identify possessive pronouns when identifying articles of clothing.
    c. Discriminate yes/no when given candy and lemon juice in a forced choice option.
    d. Sign "eat" before each bite at snack.
6. Social:
    a. Identify family members from a group of pictures.
    b. Reduce the number of tantrums by 25%.

All the measurement criteria, persons responsible, and even the space where instruction was to be completed are included. These same skills could be taught in functional routines that lead to a critical effect for the student. For example, the following skills could be included in the routine Preparing and Eating a Snack:

1. Gross motor: Pouring; walking; reaching (refrigerator, shelf, across table); carrying; placing

2. Fine motor: Cutting toast; spreading peanut butter; measuring Kool-Aid, water; setting silverware
3. Cognitive/preacademic:
   A. Colors: Orange juice, green plates, yellow glasses
   B. Numbers: 2 cups water, 5 forks, 6 spoons
   C. Letters: Cereal box, labels, placemat names
4. Self-help: Eating manners, using utensils
5. Communication: Asking for things, saying "thank you," conversation during snack, yes/no for wants more
6. Social: Serving food, asking other children if they want something, passing things

The use of functional routines to teach basic skills enables you to integrate the skills into meaningful sequences that will help students achieve their goals in various natural environments. Since your IEPs will look a little different from others your students' parents may have seen, it might be helpful to create a chart similar to the list above to show them how all the skills they expected to be taught were being integrated into functional routines. After the first IEP meeting, it probably will not be necessary to go over the skills for most parents. Since communication between parents and teachers is so important to the instructional process, it is important to anticipate the concerns of your parents during the first IEP meeting where the IMPACT curriculum is being introduced. Many parents have been taught to look for an objective or two in each of the six basic areas of child development. To ignore that history is only courting the disaster of miscommunication.

A more general comparison between the various types of curricula is shown in Table 8.1. Nonfunctional curricular elements are shown in Type 1. Type 2 reflects apparent functional curricula by including real-life objects in instruction instead of the abstract ones more often used by developmental psychologists (e.g., sorting colored blocks becomes sorting silverware). The instructional format and context, however, remain the same. Without changing the structure of instruction, little is gained by switching the objects. Type 3, the final curricular type, is a functional one. Each of the curricular areas is included in an integrated routine that achieves something for the student, which is fundamental to the IMPACT curriculum.

COMMUNICATION ROUTINES IN IEPS

As has been stated before, communication is the most important skill that can be developed in any child. IMPACT integrates communication goals into existing routines so that the language will be learned in natural contexts. This section shows you how to develop various communication programs for the various functions in language development discussed in Chapter 5 (page 24) "Language and Communication." Table 8.2 summarizes the instructional goals for each of the communication patterns listed in Chapter 5 (page 31).

Developing a Program for Children Who
Exhibit Adequate Forms, Multiple Functions

Some children with moderate to severe handicaps use adequate communicative forms to meet multiple language functions. This category most often applies to chil-

Table 8.1. Comparison between different types of curricula across curricular area goals by examining instructional elements

	Curricular area					
	Fine motor	Gross motor	Cognitive/Pre-academic	Communication	Self-help	Social
Goal:	Coordination	Coordination	Matching eye-hand coordination	Request food at table	Independence	Interaction
Curriculum Type 1: Nonfunctional—Content and context irrelevant						
Curricular element						
Task:	Snip scissors	Walk on balance beam	Stack blocks; string beads	Label food items	Name clothes	Point to picture of boy/girl
Measurement:	How far can you snip	How far/fast can you walk	How many, high, how long	Number of imitations, verbal or sign	Number of times correct or percent of steps done independently	Percent correct
Technology:	Repeated trials with assistance	Repeated trials with assistance	Repeated trials with assistance	Massed trial	Massed trial	Massed trial
Curriculum Type 2: Nonfunctional—Content improved, context artificial						
Curricular element						
Task:	Unscrew jar at table	Walk hall	Sort silverware	Request food; sign for eat	Pants off/on	Point to pictures of family
Measurement:	Number correct	Steps/minute	Percent or rate correct	Number initiated syntactic expansions	Number of times correct or percent of steps done independently	Percent correct
Technology:	Massed trial	Assistance plus reinforcement	Massed trial	Massed trial; break up meal to increase trials	Massed trial	Massed trial
Curriculum Type 3: Functional—Content and context integrated to ensure critical effect						
Curricular element						
Task:	Unscrew thermos to pour drink	Walk to restaurant or grocery store	Set table; empty dishwasher	Request food at lunch; ask for more	Dress for swimming	Pass food; prepare food; play video game
Measurement:	Amount of assistance; time required	Amount of assistance; time required	Amount of assistance; time required	Child initiations various forms	Amount of assistance; time required	Number of requests/replies; duration of activity
Technology:	Lunch routine (Includes opening peanut butter jar in lunch preparation, turning doorknobs to get to eating area, and other trials)	Various routines	Lunch, dinner, breakfast, snack routines	Various routines	Various routines	Various routines

Table 8.2.   Instructional goals for communication patterns of children with moderate to severe handicaps

Communication pattern	Instructional goals
Adequate forms, multiple functions	Refining forms
Adequate forms, limited functions	Build functions, refine existing forms
Limited forms, multiple functions	Expand forms, refine existing forms
Limited forms, limited functions	Build functions, expand forms, refine existing forms
No identifiable forms or functions	Build functions, induce forms and then refine

dren with autism and children with other severe handicaps who have developed more sophisticated communication functioning. Children in this category usually have a fairly complex verbal/symbol system. They effectively satisfy material needs and wants at home and at school. Typically, the language of such children meets several functions that allow them control over some situations in some environments. Students in this category are sometimes referred to as "high functioning." The adequacy of their communicative form is measured by how reliably it produces change in the environment, its universality, and its acceptability (see Chapter 5). For many children with moderate to severe handicaps, this level of performance is a desirable long-term goal. If your student(s) already exhibits this level of functioning, educational goals must be selected that increase sophistication of form and the number of functions, allowing access to an increased number of settings and interactions (see Table 8.3).

Common Deficits   While children in this category display communication skills that are superior to those of many of their peers with moderate to severe handicaps, they still have deficits in many communication areas. A closer look at these deficits is required before developing a comprehensive educational plan. The following deficits can be observed in children with adequate form serving multiple functions:

1.   Inappropriate sentence structure including problems with grammar, pronouns, question versus statement markers, and word choice
2.   Lack of communication skills required in the community; these include:
     a.   Learning community phrases
     b.   Verbal etiquette
     c.   Following group directions
3.   Insufficient number of functions

These deficits limit the child's ability to enter many settings, thereby decreasing the potential for interaction. Improvement in these skill areas will increase independent functioning by building sufficient communicative control across settings.

Increasing Form Sophistication   Increasing a child's form sophistication will increase the ability of others to understand his or her intent. This is accomplished primarily by increasing a child's accuracy of sentence formation or sentence structure. Elements of sentence structure to be considered are grammar, pronouns, the use of questions versus statements, word choice, and word order. Inappropriate sentence structure is commonly observed in verbal children with autism and other moderate to severe handicaps. They will frequently ask a question when a statement is required, or make a statement when trying to ask a question. Pronoun reversal and the inappropriate use of third person pronouns are also frequent errors.

The following are examples of inappropriate sentence structure commonly used:

Table 8.3. Communication instructional guidelines for children with adequate forms, multiple functions

Common deficiencies	Goal and program emphasis
Lack of socially appropriate communication skills, verbal etiquette, appropriate withholding of verbal response, community phrases	Increase social communication abilities, including withholding inappropriate verbal behavior
Inappropriate sentence structure: grammar, pronouns, questions, statements, word choice	Increase form sophistication while keeping function intact
Incomplete number of functions, usually higher level social or conversational functions missing	Increase number of functions

1. *Inappropriate use of question markers*
   Inappropriate: Did we go camping last summer?
   Appropriate: We went camping last summer.
2. *Inappropriate use of statement*
   Inappropriate: Is it milk and cookies for my lunch today.
   Appropriate: I have milk and cookies in my lunch today.
3. *Pronoun reversal*
   Inappropriate: Tickle you.
   Appropriate: Tickle me.
   Inappropriate: You want to go outside.
   Appropriate: I want to go outside.
4. *Use of third person pronouns*
   Inappropriate: He wants a cookie, doesn't he?
   Appropriate: I want a cookie.

Educators and parents of children with autism often become accustomed to hearing these grammatical errors. Familiarity with the child's communication may permit accurate interpretation of incorrect statements in the home and classroom environment, but these grammatical errors will hinder acceptability and control in community settings. Even though grammar is not a major concern for children who have limited communicative control, it is an important goal for students who are "high functioning."

Communication Skills Required in the Community   Learning phrases that are required to interact with people in the community facilitates independent functioning and increases the child's ability to enter different environments. Children who have adequate forms for multiple functions may have adequate vocabulary to operate at home and at school but seldom have sufficient vocabulary to operate in community settings. Required communications skills for community functioning consist of those determined by the context of the settings or those that increase social acceptability in community settings.

1. Learning Community Phrases   You can provide training in certain vocabulary items in conjunction with community skills to facilitate communicative control and independence across settings. Skills required in community settings are determined by the setting itself. For example, independent functioning in restaurants requires the ability to order food or to request a seat or your bill. Buying goods in a department store requires a different set of verbal skills, such as requesting assistance, locating items, requesting the price of an item, and responding to a clerk's questions. In each of these examples, the required communication skills are dictated by the setting. Surveying those settings a child currently has access to and those the parents want him or her to enter will determine appropriate instructional content to remediate these deficiencies.

2. *Verbal Etiquette*   Another communication skill required in most settings is verbal etiquette. This includes manners (e.g., "excuse me," "please," and "thank you"), getting someone's attention in an appropriate way, waiting your turn in a conversation, following the topic being discussed, and withholding inappropriate verbal behavior. Improving verbal etiquette will enhance the acceptability of your students.

3. *Following Group Directions*   Another goal for these students might be to increase their ability to recognize themselves as part of a group. These children may be able to follow instructional commands directed to them individually but seldom respond to cues directed towards the group. In the classroom, group directions usually occur during periods when the whole class is moving from one place to another (e.g., classroom to lunchroom) or during a group game. In the community, group directions may be given by a bus driver, police officer, or food server. Identifying commonly occurring group directions across settings will aid in the development of appropriate educational content items.

4. *Increasing Function*   The final area of concern is building additional intent. While children who are high functioning demonstrate basic communication skills, they seldom exhibit a full range of functions. After reviewing the number of functions currently met, you should select for instruction those additional functions that will produce meaningful changes in the child's life. For those children with very few functions, you will want to select those functions that are utilitarian, such as protesting, responding to others, and intiating contact with people in their environment. With those children who have most of the utilitarian functions in place, you may focus on the more sophisticated ones, such as maintaining a conversation and asking about things in their environment.

In summary, when developing comprehensive educational plans for children who exhibit adequate forms and multiple function use, emphasis should be placed on sophistication of current form and increasing the number of functions. This will ensure access to a wide range of settings and interactions.

Developing a Program for Children with Adequate Forms, Limited Functions

Children with adequate forms and limited functions are usually children whose verbal behavior includes grammatically correct sentences or phrases but whose language is rarely used communicatively. Even though the form may be understandable, universal, and acceptable to others, the intent of their language is lost on the receiver. These children have been described as having language without communication. The ability to meet communication functions varies from one child to the next. That is, some children may use their language capabilities more communicatively than others, but their major deficiency is their inability to use their current form to satisfy multiple functions. On initial observation, these children may appear to be competent users of language. In fact, they are often the most puzzling to assess. They often say complete sentences with content that could be communicative in the right context. A closer look at the content of each utterance *in the context* in which it is used suggests otherwise. The content, even when it appears to be appropriate, is usually out of context or irrelevant to the situation. It may also appear bizarre in nature or be nonsensical. A child might say, for example, "There's a hydroplane on top of the space needle." Often the same utterance is repeated many times for days on end. Often teachers and parents will listen for the one time in a hundred that the utterance may have an environmental referent. A consistent connection between the content and the context, however, is hard to identify. Sometimes the content may include novel information or be echoic. While evidence exists that echoic responses may be used communicatively by some children, the communicative value of each response is often difficult to determine.

The primary goal of educational programming for these children (see Table 8.4) is to increase their ability to use current forms more communicatively, that is, to increase the number of functions utilizing current forms. This requires restructuring the environment to increase the need for communicative intent, reinforcing the child's attempts to communicate, and ignoring the child's noncommunicative verbal behavior. Special attention must be given to the relevant contextual features of each utterance you will provide training for the child to use. Children with adequate form and limited function must learn to select content items that are relevant to the situation. In some cases it may be helpful to build additional nonverbal communicative behaviors, such as gestures, while providing training in the communicative use of verbal behavior.

A child who is nonverbal can also display adequate form even if the number of functions is limited. For example, if a child uses a gesture to request desired objects, then you can train the child in an additional gesture to allow him or her to protest an undesired object. This builds the child's current form and satisfies an additional function, thereby increasing control over the environment. Programming should not concentrate on increasing form sophistication until these children are able to show sufficient communicative control over their environment. Emphasizing or training in form complexity before a child has sufficient ability to use communicative functions defeats the purpose of functional skills training. Increasing each student's ability to function effectively should always be the major goal of programming.

Developing a Program for Children with Limited or Idiosyncratic Forms, Multiple Functions

Children who have limited forms and multiple functions are frequently able to operate in some environments, but their use of a limited form seriously restricts their ability to operate in new or unfamiliar settings. The more limited the form, the more limited the child's audience will be. Children in this category typically use a single form (e.g., as pointing, tantruming) to fulfill multiple functions, or have developed inappropriate or idiosyncratic communicative patterns. Often the behavior used is one that has acquired meaning to one or more members of the family through repeated trials.

Table 8.4. Communication instructional guidelines for children with adequate forms, limited functions

Common deficiencies	Goal and program emphasis
Inability to express intent across environments, people, or materials	Increase number of functions utilizing current forms; increase sophistication of current forms, keeping all functions intact; continue to build additional functions

When a child uses a limited or idiosyncratic form, others involved in the interaction must use contextual cues to interpret the child's intent. These children may be easily understood by teachers and parents but have little or no effect when conveying messages to others. Only those persons who are significantly interested in the child's communication will take the time or make the effort to determine the communicative intent of most of these children. Instructional efforts for these children (see Table 8.5) should emphasize improving the acceptability and/or universality of the existing forms and increasing the diversity of forms available to the student. It is important to remember that while you are building an acceptable form you always need to keep the communicative functions intact.

For children with appropriate but limited forms, teachers must identify which of the present forms can be shaped into more sophisticated ones and determine which functions will require learning new forms. If a child communicates using a single gesture, then this gesture can be shaped into a series of signs that will discriminate different communicative functions. Initially, each function could have a different sign. After the child learned to reliably use each sign to discriminate each function, then more sophisticated signing could be taught. Shaping current forms may be more efficient than providing training in a form that is new to the child. Adding a new system at the expense of the current one may disrupt the child's present ability to meet multiple functions through communication.

If your student currently meets communicative functions using inappropriate or idiosyncratic behaviors, you may also be able to replace these with more appropriate or easily understood forms. Identify the suspected communicative intent for each inappropriate behavior and determine if there is an alternate appropriate, communicative behavior that can be shaped from that form, or whether or not another form will have to be substituted. Perhaps the child throws a tantrum in order to get something. Often it is impossible to shape portions of a tantrum into more acceptable forms. Many times there are, however, signals that precede the actual tantrum that could be used as a beginning sign. Suppose a child wants to communicate that he or she does not want to do some assignment. The child jumps to the floor, grabs the teacher's leg, and begins biting. At this point, there is little to shape into a more appropriate communicative form. After carefully watching the child, it is discovered that he or she begins to tap the table just before leaping out of the chair. This tapping can be used to shape a communicative form: When the first few taps occur, the teacher quickly shapes a simple sign for "no" or "stop", then releases the child, and leaves the area for a short time. Since the new form is successful and much easier to use than jumping to the floor and biting, it effectively competes with the biting. The student has now learned a new sign for "stop" or "no". This use of effective shaping of predecessor movements can be a very effective teaching tool.

Table 8.5.   Communication instructional guidelines for children with limited forms, multiple functions

Common deficiencies	Goal and program emphasis
Idiosyncratic or inappropriate forms that are difficult to respond to and therefore not usually reinforced	Shape increasingly sophisticated form, keeping functions intact
Limited audience due to inappropriate or idiosyncratic form	If unacceptable form is used, replace with easily acquired form while keeping current functions intact
Lack of full range of functions	Increase number of functions

Sometimes the behavior(s) exhibited by the child may make it difficult to determine exactly what the child wants. In order to make the child's intent understandable, you could take the child's hand and have him or her point to the object or activity you think is your best guess. If the child indicates that you are correct, you have a starting point for shaping a more universal form. If no communicative form exists, then select one that can be taught easily and will keep the child's functions intact. Reaching or pointing are probably the easiest in which to train the child. Once your student begins to reliably express communicative intent(s) using acceptable form, he or she can begin to receive instruction in form complexity or sophistication. Again, it is very important to keep the existing communicative functions intact throughout the training process. Too much attention to refining the form, or substituting standard signs, or training in vocal imitations at the expense of communication will not increase the child's ability to influence what happens to him or her or improve his or her independent functioning. Also, while these children have multiple functions, they still do not have a full range of functions. You will want to provide training to increase the number of functions.

Developing a Program for Children with Limited Forms, Limited Functions

Children with limited form and limited functions have communicative behaviors that are hard to identify. They rarely display more than the most basic functions, and the forms they employ are limited. The forms used may be acceptable or unacceptable, but in all cases they will be used sparingly for a limited set of communicative intents. For example, the child may point or gesture appropriately, but use the communicative form only in order to satisfy immediate needs and wants. He or she does not use this form on any other occasion. The form, in this case, is acceptable, but the child uses it to satisfy so few functions that its usefulness is not realized.

Often the form may be viewed as unacceptable or idiosyncratic and only understood by persons who have had a great deal of contact with the student. An unacceptable form such as crying or whining may serve more than one function, such as satisfying needs and wants and also protesting, but because of its negative effects it may go unrewarded by people other than those most closely associated with the child. The same is true for idiosyncratic forms since virtually no one outside the child's immediate environment will recognize the child's communicative effort. For example, a child might stand in front of a desired object and stare at it. You, as the child's teacher, may recognize the child's intent, but it is likely to be ignored by people less familiar with the child.

Educational planning (see Table 8.6) for a child who has limited forms and limited functions should focus on training in additional functions and shaping the undesired

Table 8.6. Communication instructional guidelines for children with limited forms, limited functions

Common deficiencies	Goal and program emphasis
Inability to meet basic functions	Increase number of functions using current form (if acceptable)
Form that is difficult to respond to and unlikely to be reinforced	If unacceptable or idiosyncratic form is used, replace with easily acquired form first with current functions, while adding new functions
Limited audience	Shape increasingly sophisticated form, keeping current functions intact

forms to ones that are more acceptable. If the child has an acceptable form, such as gesturing or pointing, then training in functions will be your first priority before training in additional forms or shaping a more sophisticated form. If the child's form is unacceptable or too idiosyncratic, you will have to shape a simple form that is easy to provide training in, such as reaching, that will enable the child to fulfill each of the existing functions *while you begin to provide training in new functions*. You might, in fact, want to start with shaping any existing functions so that you can strengthen the instruction within a context that is already familiar to the child. Your primary goal is, as always, to keep the child's existing communicative functions intact whenever you want to shape new or increasingly sophisticated forms or introduce a new function. When you select a new function to teach, the form you use to teach it should be simple, easy to provide training in, and fulfill the new communicative function for the child. Any form that does not fulfill the desired function is useless because it is not paired with a meaningful intent.

Developing a Program for Children with No Identifiable Forms or Functions

Children who have no identifiable forms or functions are usually passive in all environments and seem to let the world flow around them. They often are very withdrawn and may spend most of their time engaged in stereotypic behavior. They are children with no identifiable communicative form and who show little intent to control the environment. Rather than acting on their environment, they let the environment act on them. The will wait until they are fed, wait until someone takes them to the bathroom, and wait until they are allowed a break from work, if they will work at all. Being alone seems to be their most preferred activity. Because of this, reinforcers for communicative functions and forms are often hard to find.

Developing a communication program for these children (see Table 8.7) requires restructuring the environment, building a need for communicative intent, and providing the child with a form that will produce immediate results when used in the environment. Also, train the child in additional communicative intent when the first intent the child exhibits is being reliably produced. Communicative intent can be facilitated by rearranging the environment. Putting a child's favorite toys and foods out of reach means that the child must request assistance to get them. Placing two children in proximity at a table or in a play area increases the likelihood of peer interaction, or the need to communicate wanting to be left alone. Classrooms with small children are often set up allowing children access to materials, toys, and so forth. While some adaptations of the classroom environment aid independence (e.g., lowering coat hooks so children can reach them), those same adaptations may hinder communication with children with no identifiable forms or functions. If children who have

Table 8.7. Communication instructional guidelines for children with no identifiable forms or functions

Common deficiencies	Goal and program emphasis
Extreme withdrawal	Restructure environment to build need for intent
Little or no active participation in or control of environment	Teach an acceptable form that is simple enough to give immediate control
Seriously deficient interaction and communication	Provide training in additional functions when first function can be produced reliably

no identifiable communication are allowed access to all activities and preferred objects, there is little need for them to interact. It is important to remember that most adaptations to the environment made to facilitate the independent functioning of communicative children may have the opposite effect with these children. A balance between teaching those skills that will generalize outside of the classroom, where things are not arranged for the convenience of children, and inducing communicative attempts, will have to be struck. For any classroom modification that is made, teachers should consider the potential effect such adaptations may have on the communication of all the children in the classroom.

SELECTING THE APPROPRIATE FORM

Another critical educational decision you will have to make when writing your IEP is the selection of a communicative form that is appropriate for the child. There is no single communication system that will be appropriate for all children. The critical concern is selecting a set of forms for communication that can be used by the student to achieve the desired communicative intent(s). At the same time, the form(s) selected must be understood by a majority of the people in the student's environment. Obviously, if the form you select is only understood by the teaching staff and a few others, it will have limited utility outside the training environment. The communication systems that have the most universality, however, often are too difficult to master soon enough to ensure their communicative intent. A delicate balance between being communicative and being understood by others needs to be developed. You will need to continually monitor your communication selections several times during the school year to ensure that the communicative intent is being achieved throughout the instructional process. Training in a form for future communicative intent is never very successful and should not become common practice.

Children who are nonverbal and are unable to acquire verbal skills often receive training in sign language. Unfortunately, these systems may not be effective for some of these children. Signs, or some approximation of them, may be selected as the instructional form if they serve to achieve a communication function for the child. If this is not possible, then another set of forms will need to be developed, such as gestures or communication boards. Automatically selecting sign language as the form for training, without consideration of communicative intent and the possible use of other forms, is a very common mistake. Consideration should be given to all possible alternative forms.

Another concern before selecting a communicative form for instruction is the child's potential for learning that form. You will need to look at how closely the alternative resembles behavior the child currently uses, how long you think it will take to train the child in the alternative form, and how potentially effective the form may be. For children who do not use an adequate form (i.e., one that is acceptable to others around her or him), a form must be shaped from existing forms or replaced by a more effective one that will provide them with immediate control.

Any alternate communication system will limit, to some extent, the number of people with whom the child can interact. Some are more limiting than others. For example, Blissymbols limit the child to communicating only with others who know that same system. This is more limiting than pointing to pictures, while pointing to pictures is more limiting than verbal speech. Even though verbal speech is the most universal, it is frequently the most difficult form in which to provide training. If acquiring verbal skills is likely for your student, you may want to simultaneously train him or her in an additional form, such as gesture or signing, to increase the immediate communicative ability of your student. This will address some of the child's immediate needs while you work toward the acquisition of verbal behavior.

When determining which communication form is appropriate for your student, you should consider the student's ability to use visual, auditory, manual, and oral modalities. If your student cannot attend to or easily discriminate pictures or printed materials, then picture books, Blissymbols, and so forth are probably inappropriate. Your goal should always be to give the child immediate communicative control over his or her environment. The amount of extra instructional time it takes to provide training in a system that requires tool skills (White, 1980) that the child does not have will work against that goal. Similarly, sign language would be inappropriate for children with poor motor control, and responding to verbal commands would be inappropriate for children with poor auditory discrimination.

Children who are noncommunicative will learn to control their environment only if they are provided with a system that they can handle and where a majority of their communicative attempts are acknowledged. When determining the communication form that is most appropriate for your student, select the form that is least limiting and will produce the most immediate results.

When selecting an appropriate communication system for your student, you should consider these four questions: 1) how will the system you select limit the child's audience, 2) are there any behaviors your student currently has in his or her repertoire that can be shaped for purposes of communication, 3) how acceptable is the form you choose to other persons in the child's environment, 4) how portable is the system? Table 7.3, the summary of instructional goals for communication patterns discussed in this section, can be used along with the Home and School Inventory Summary Sheets to assist you in programming for each child. After making the considerations discussed above, use the IMPACT Communication Form Selection Summary Sheet on page 67 to select the probable forms in which to provide instruction.

WRITING THE IEP

At this juncture you should have completed the Home and School Inventories, set your priorities based on parental input and professional judgement, selected the skill areas you will be teaching, determined the instructional situations you will use for instruction, and decided upon the communication functions and forms you will be integrating into your functional routines. These data are then combined into a functional IEP using whatever format is developed by your school. The traditional summary of present levels of performance becomes the inventory summary sheets. The goals and objectives become the instructional routines. Placement decisions are instructional decisions based on the routines and instructional situations selected. Communication, physical, and occupational therapies become integrated into functional routines rather than being pull-out programs that need to be scheduled throughout the day. Criteria of performance become the achieving of desired critical effects with the level of independence that has been decided on by the multidisciplinary team. In most cases, functioning in the natural setting independently or with prosthetic supervision will be the goal of instruction.

IMPACT COMMUNICATION
FORM SELECTION SUMMARY SHEET

Name: _____   Date: _____

Enter the form(s) selected for each of the functions listed below. The forms listed here should be the desired forms that you intend to include in your IEP goals and objectives. You may choose to use the same form with different activities within the same general function. For example, you may want to develop a two-word sentence for the ask function. The one form used to ask would be the same in all three ask functions listed on the sheet.

Function	Form (describe)
Ask, food	
Ask, activity	
Ask, outside	
Indicate injury	
Help, get things	
Help, find things	
Help, do something	
Ask directions	
Protest, activity	
Protest, food	
Protest, object	
Respond, family	
Respond, adults	
Respond, peers	
Initiate interaction, family	
Initiate interaction, adults	
Initiate interaction, peers	
Continue interaction, family	
Continue interaction, adults	
Continue interaction, peers	
Seek affection	
Seek reward	
Express interest	
Relate past events	
Pretend, Fantasy	

When completed, a functional IEP becomes the road map for a longitudinal, functional, age-appropriate program for children with moderate to severe handicaps. The amount of effort expended in preparing a functional IEP will provide enormous dividends in terms of effective and efficient instructional programming. Once the initial IEP is written, then subsequent IEP meetings will consist of modifications of the current plan along with additions that reflect changing environmental needs of the child.

3

Learning with IMPACT

9 The Instructional Process

Part 2 of this handbook described in some detail the process through which a functional curriculum may be developed for each of your students. This chapter describes a set of procedures for teaching skills that have been identified as instructional targets through application of that curriculum development process. A great many texts are available that define, describe, and discuss research related to instructional principles applicable to students with moderate to severe handicaps. It is not our purpose to provide yet another overview of such principles. In fact, we assume you are already familiar with most common behavioral principles and terms (e.g., positive reinforcement, shaping, schedules of reinforcement, generalization, prompting) and with many ways to apply those principles effectively. Our intent is to illustrate an integrated set of procedures in which those principles, and student performance data, can be employed within natural contexts to teach functional skills as complete routines rather than as a collection of discrete components. The information presented here is not intended to replace your current knowledge of best practices; rather, it is meant to be used in conjunction with that knowledge as you implement the IMPACT instructional process.

You will need some tools before you actually begin instruction. These include task-analyzed routines, a data system that will reflect changes in critical skill elements, and an assessment procedure that has specific and direct implications for teaching. Procedures for providing training in skills as routines, evaluating student performance, making decisions based on data, and facilitating generalization and maintenance are then presented. Throughout the discussion, forms and data collection sheets that will help you plan and implement instruction will be introduced.

DEVELOPING TASK ANALYSES OF ROUTINES

After routines for each child have been selected, instructional programs are developed. The first step in this process is to task analyze each routine into a series of steps that lead to the critical effect or outcome (e.g., eating: hunger reduction, toileting: elimination). Task analysis refers to the identification and sequencing of component skills within the routine. When you perform a task analysis, you are determining those specific behaviors (or subgroups of behaviors) that the learner is required to perform in order to gain the critical effect. In addition, you are indicating the order in which you feel those behaviors should be performed so that the effect will be achieved efficiently and reliably.

The process begins with the identification of the starting and ending points of the routine. The first step should be identifying the task-related behavior that immediately follows the natural cue for performance of the routine within nontraining situations. The term natural cue refers to the information an individual typically receives in natural environments before an action is performed (Falvey, Brown, Lyon, Baumgart, & Schroeder, 1980). Natural cues could include, for example, a request to "Come to dinner," arrival at the corner of a controlled intersection, an alarm going off in the morning, or the price of an item stated by a cashier. Each of those cues should be immediately followed by a different and appropriate behavior. The first step following a request to "Come to dinner," for example, could be to begin movement toward the dining area, while the step following arrival at the corner of a controlled intersection could be to look at the signal. (See Falvey et al. [1980], for a thorough discussion of the concept of natural cues.)

The final step in the analysis should be identifying the behavior that precedes achievement of the routine's critical effect. In a communicative interaction, for example, the critical effect might be receipt of a requested item. The final step, then, might be pointing to an appropriate picture in a communication book. The critical effect of putting on a jacket is usually going outdoors. Completing the act of zipping up the jacket would then be an appropriate final step.

It should be noted that a basic difference between traditional task analyses and analyses of routines lies in the determination of the end point. In traditional analyses, the skill sequence usually ends when the task has been accomplished from the *instructor's* point of view. The analysis of a routine, however, terminates when the step has been performed that allows attainment of the critical effect by the *learner*. A traditional task analysis designed for use in a program to teach a student to obtain food and eat at a fast food restaurant, for example, might list "cleans up and deposits tray" as the last step. Certainly, cleaning up and depositing the tray is the last thing most of us do before we leave the restaurant. However, 1) it is not a behavior that one must perform in order to eat at a fast food restaurant, and 2) the critical effect we achieve for that behavior is quite subtle and depends on considerable social awareness. The most powerful effect available in the restaurant is likely to be reduction of hunger which, of course, is satisfied through the behaviors necessary to eat the meal. Therefore, to be most useful as an instructional tool, the task analysis for the Get and Eat Food at Fast Food Restaurant routine should end with eating behaviors, not cleaning up and depositing the tray. If it is felt that cleaning up and depositing the tray is really a necessary skill for the student to learn, it should be considered as a separate routine for which some critical effect will have to be arranged.

Once starting and ending points have been identified, the teacher must determine those steps that fall in between and their sequence within the routine. The size and number of steps depends on both the current abilities of the student and the complexity of the task. If a student has few behaviors in his or her repertoire and is, therefore, likely to require considerable teacher assistance to complete a routine, more steps of smaller size will be required to permit the instructor to accurately assess student progress and make good instructional decisions. For a student who requires a great deal of assistance with a lunch routine, a single step labeled "removes food from lunch box" may be too large if he or she needs help opening the lunch box, removing the food, opening the thermos, and getting the food out of sacks and containers. In such a case, the single step might be broken into four separate steps. More and smaller steps may also be needed if a task performance requires many dissimilar behaviors, a variety of fine discriminations, or a sequence of responses that seem unrelated to one another.

On the other hand, if you know a student can perform several consecutive steps independently, you can collapse them into one. If, for example, a student can respond to the cue that it is time for recess by getting his or her coat and getting in line at the door independently, those actions can be collapsed into "prepares to go" rather than two separate steps. This will save you time as well as help focus on those areas where the student is most lacking in skill.

If the completed task analysis consists of more than 15 steps, you may want to divide one routine into several different routines or subroutines. On a purely practical level, we have observed that instructors frequently have trouble managing routines (e.g., delivering prompts as planned, collecting data) when the number of steps exceeds approximately 15. The management problems that could accompany a 50 or 55 step Lunchtime routine might, for example, be reduced by dividing the lunch into three routines: Preparing for Lunch, Eating Lunch, and Cleaning Up after Lunch. Note that each routine permits access to its own critical effect. Preparing for Lunch results in access to food, Eating Lunch results in hunger reduction, and Cleaning Up after Lunch could result in any of a number of effects. In schools, a critical effect that is typically available after lunch is the opportunity to go outside to play. At home, that same effect is frequently available.

Of perhaps greater consequence than the management issue, however, is that students often engage in behaviors (e.g., aggression, stereotypies) that disrupt performance of the routine when a large number of responses must be emitted before getting to the critical effect. Limiting the number of steps to 15 permits the student to achieve the effect with a reasonable expenditure of time and effort.

Such a limitation should also compel the instructor to consider the need to develop interim critical effects; that is, effects that will follow the performance of subroutines during initial stages of training. For example, a natural critical effect may not follow the first 15 steps of a 28-step Bedroom Cleanup routine. Therefore, in order to reduce the probability that the student will engage in competing, disruptive behaviors, some critical effect for completion of those first 15 steps should be arranged by the instructor. Perhaps a break would serve the purpose. Later in training, when the student is more proficient, it will probably be possible to group several steps together and combine the resulting subroutine with the other steps to result in a single Cleanup routine of 15 steps or fewer, which is followed by a natural critical effect (e.g., being allowed to go to the dining room for breakfast).

CHARACTERISTICS OF A DATA COLLECTION SYSTEM FOR ROUTINES

Data collected on student performance during initial assessments as well as during instruction reflect changes in the critical elements of skills as they are performed in context. Critical elements include both the extent to which the student is able to function without being assisted by other persons (e.g., parents and teachers) and the length of time required to initiate and perform a skill. Together, they influence the child's ability to effectively operate in various environments.

Assistance by Others

A student who always requires considerable physical assistance to perform some task, is obviously more limited in coping with environmental demands than a student who responds to more natural cues for performance. During assessment, therefore, an attempt is made to collect data that indicate the type of assistance needed by the student to successfully perform each step in the routine. Then, during instruction, similar data collection practices are employed to help the teacher decide when to reduce assistance and thereby move the student closer to independent functioning.

Speed of Performance

If the pupil takes an abnormally long time to respond to a cue or completes a task very slowly, it is unlikely that skills will be maintained or that they will generalize to non-training situations. Slow performance of trained behaviors often results in: 1) the task being completed by others who become impatient, 2) the failure of the student to receive natural consequences that follow fluent performance, and/or 3) the use of competing, undesirable behaviors instead of the trained behaviors (see Barrett, 1979; Billingsley & Liberty, 1982; Horner & Billingsley, 1988). For example, a student who can put on a coat, but takes 30 minutes to do so, will not be allowed to use that skill. Someone will grow impatient with the child and simply help him or her to put the coat on. In addition, it is likely that performing the skill so slowly will delay the critical effect of being ready to go outside for such a long time that the child will engage in inappropriate behaviors (e.g., throwing the coat on the floor), which will "motivate" others to do the job as quickly as possible. Such outcomes greatly reduce the functionality of any routine.

Due to the critical nature of fluent skill performance, a consistent framework for timing routines must be employed. Response latencies should be timed for each step of each routine during all assessment and instructional trials. The duration of each step should also be noted during the initial assessment of a routine to ensure that the child can perform all steps within a reasonable time. Only those steps that are not performed within the specified duration during assessment will be timed during instruction. Twice a month, however, entire routines should be timed to confirm that a reasonable duration is maintained as the child moves toward independence. In addition, the total routine should be timed when all steps have been acquired with the appropriate maximum degree of independence. If duration becomes a problem, instructional strategies to remediate the problem will need to be employed. Targeting duration for instructional intervention is covered in the "Decision Rules Applied" section of this chapter (p. 90).

ASSESSMENT PROCEDURES

Before the instructional plan is written, the student's present performance level on each step of the targeted routine must be assessed. This, of course, requires that the task analysis of the routine be prepared. One potential analysis of a Bus to Classroom routine consisting of 12 steps is shown in the Assessment Data Sheet (Figure 9.1) for a hypothetical student named Gary. Note that not only are physical skill requirements specified in the task analysis, but embedded social communication targets are also included at their appropriate positions within the skill sequence.

Defining Important Response Characteristics

Following completion of the task analysis, determine the maximum allowable duration for performance of the entire routine under natural cue and reinforcement conditions. Then, for each *step* of the task analysis:

1. *Determine the allowable latency.* Latency is measured from the presentation of the cue until the pupil begins to respond. Appropriate latencies are often determined to be from 2–5 seconds.
2. *Determine the allowable duration.* Duration, which should be measured from the beginning of the response until the completion of the step, will vary according to task requirements. For example, a shorter duration will be appropriate for "picks up lunchbox" than for "walks to classroom" in the Bus to Classroom routine.
3. *Determine the correct response form.* For each step in the routine you must decide what constitutes an acceptable behavior. For example, when Gary "exits bus," must he walk down the bus steps one at a time in order for the response form to be correct, or is he permitted to skip steps or jump to the ground?

The routine and step related factors indicated above can usually be determined by a teacher's dry run through the routine prior to assessment. Perform the routine yourself, or collect data on someone else performing the skill. Appropriate individuals for the dry run might include an aide, a volunteer, or a student who already performs the routine fluently. In addition to appropriate latencies, durations, and response forms, the dry run should also tell you whether the sequence of steps in the task analysis is correct (e.g., setting the table before getting lunch would generally be easier than getting lunch, then setting the table), and whether all necessary steps have been included.

Assessing Performance

Following the dry run and any revisions to the task analysis, take the student through the routine, allowing him or her the opportunity to respond independently in the presence of the natural cue. If the student does not begin to respond independently within the predetermined latency period, provide assistance in the form of a verbal prompt. If the student still does not respond, systematically offer other types of assistance until the child performs the behavior. Should the student perform an incorrect form of the behavior, rather than simply failing to respond, stop the response and immediately offer another type of assistance. (For a description of a similar assessment procedure, see Knapczyk [1975].)

As the above discussion indicates, prompts are provided in what is typically called an increasing assistance (or least-to-most) fashion (Billingsley & Romer, 1983; Wolery & Gast, 1984) during assessment. It should be noted, however, that this method is used during instruction only under a very limited set of conditions. When

Assessment Data Sheet

FIGURE 9.1

Manager: _____ Helen _____

Name: _____ Gary _____

Date: _____

Routine: _____ Bus to Classroom _____

Beginning natural cue: _____ Teacher approaches Gary _____

Critical effect: _____ Participation in classroom activities _____

Latency: _____ 3 seconds _____ Duration of routine: _____ 3 min., 10 sec. _____

[Note: Includes 3 seconds latency for each step.]

Types of assistance:
- FP = Full physical assistance
- PA = Partial physical assistance
- G = Gestural cue
- V = Directive verbal cue
- I = Natural cue or independent
- Ⓒ = Communication target

Steps	Duration	Date	Date	Date	Date	Type of assistance for instruction (describe)
1. Ⓒ Requests help with seatbelt	2 sec	FP	FP	FP	V/FP	Say "Show me 'help.'" Mold sign for "help."
2. Walks down aisle	15 sec	V	V	V	V	"Go to class."
3. Picks up lunch box or other materials	10 sec	I	V(ED)	I	I	[Note: No duration errors occurred with type of assistance selected for instruction.]
4. Exits bus	5 sec	PA	I	I	I	I
5. Walks to building entry	35 sec	PA	PA	PA	PA	Hold his hand while walking
6. Ⓒ Requests help with door	2 sec	FP	PA	FP	V/FP	Say "Show me 'help.'" Mold sign for "help."
7. Enters building	2 sec	PA	PA	PA	PA	Hold his hand while entering building
8. Walks to classroom	60 sec	PA	FP	PA	PA	Hold his hand while walking
9. Puts away lunch box and other materials	10 sec	PA	G	FP	FP	Take his hands and guide to shelf
10. Takes off coat	7 sec	I(ED)	I	I(ED)	I	[Note: Record duration errors during instruction.]
11. Ⓒ Requests help finding hook	2 sec	FP	FP	FP	V/FP	Say "Show me 'help.'" Mold sign for "help."
12. Hangs up coat	4 sec	G	PA	V	4th trial, G	G — Point at hook

instruction is provided, procedures designed to ensure that students make a high proportion of correct to incorrect responses in the presence of natural cues are employed.

Types of Assistance

Figure 9.2 suggests several types of assistance that might be employed as well as a possible order of sequential application. For example, the eighth step listed on the Assessment Data Sheet for the Bus to Classroom routine is "walks to classroom." The teacher has specified an allowable latency of 3 seconds. The student, therefore, is given 3 seconds from the time he enters the building to begin walking to the classroom independently. If he does not begin in 3 seconds, the teacher provides a verbal cue (e.g., "Go to the classroom"). If there is no response during the next 3 seconds, the teacher provides a gestural cue. Additional types of assistance continue to be provided until the pupil does begin walking to the classroom. In this example, the response was finally initiated within the allowable latency period following partial physical assistance (i.e., the teacher held the pupil's hand while walking).

Recording Assessment Data

On the Assessment Data Sheet, record either that the student performed independently (I) or indicate the type and precise nature of assistance required on each step. It should be emphasized that independent responding may occur following auditory, visual, or physical cues that are customarily present in the natural environment. Parents, for example, usually call their children to the table for dinner (a verbal cue). Because the children are not expected to arrive at the table when any lesser degree of assistance is provided, the verbal cue represents maximum desired independence. In addition, totally independent performance of a particular step may be impossible due to a student's severe physical limitations, but partial participation (Baumgart et al., 1982) in the activity is possible if assistance is provided. When a response to some type of assistance represents the sort of functional independence described above, score "I" during assessment [and instructional data collection (see Figure 9.3)] and indicate the type of assistance provided, for example, I-V (i.e., independent-verbal). This score indicates that, although antecedent cues are provided by another individual, no additional training needs to be conducted to further reduce assistance.

AUDITORY OR VISUAL ASSISTANCE

1. **Directive verbal cue (V)** The teacher gives only a verbal direction (or some alternative mode of communication). In a Handwashing routine, if the student failed to approach the sink independently, the teacher might provide a cue such as, "Go to the sink."

2. **Gestural cue (G)** A gesture or demonstration that provides information regarding the nature of the required response is provided. For example, the teacher might point toward the sink.

PHYSICAL ASSISTANCE

3. **Partial physical assistance (PA)** Part of the student's physical movement is molded by the teacher. The teacher, therefore, might orient the student toward the sink and/or guide him a step or two toward the sink.

4. **Full physical assistance (FP)** The physical movement of the student is completely molded by the teacher. As much physical assistance as necessary would be provided to move the student to the sink.

Figure 9.2. Types of assistance suggested for use during assessment and a recommended sequence for presentation.

In addition to recording independent responding or the type of assistance required, the duration of the response should be timed. If the duration is longer than that specified as allowable, a duration error (ED) is recorded. The use of these duration data will be discussed under the "Decision Rules Applied" section (page 90) of this chapter.

Selecting Types of Assistance for Instruction

Because the performance of students with moderate to severe handicaps, particularly those with autism, is often variable, it is suggested that the assessment procedure be repeated three times. This may be especially important for teachers who have little experience with the child they are assessing. The type of assistance most frequently required on each step in order to produce the desired response within the allowable latency is entered and described on the Assessment Data Sheet and will become part of the criteria for a correct response during programming. On the "walks to classroom" step of the Bus to Classroom routine, partial physical assistance was required on two assessment trials and full physical assistance on the other trial. The criteria for a correct response on that step would, therefore, be: "walks to classroom within a 3 second latency and a duration of no more than 60 seconds with partial physical assistance." The most frequently required type of assistance is used to increase the chances that the student will make correct responses during instruction and, as a result, achieve positive consequences on a regular basis.

It is possible that a different type of assistance will evoke the desired response on each assessment trial. That is, on the first trial, the pupil may perform with a gestural cue, on the next with partial physical assistance, and on the third with a verbal cue. In such a situation, as in the case of the last step in the Bus to Classroom routine (i.e., "hangs up coat"), collect data on one additional trial. This can be accomplished by taking the student through the routine using the types of assistance selected for use during instruction on all steps except those to be tested. If, following the additional trial, a most frequently required type of assistance still cannot be identified, it is recommended that the form of assistance that appears to provide the greatest degree of teacher direction be employed during initial instructional sessions to ensure frequent receipt of positive consequences.

Based on the variable assessment results cited above, therefore, one additional "hangs up coat" trial was provided. Since Gary responded following a gesture, that type of prompt was selected for use in instructional sessions because it was most frequent. If, however, full physical assistance had been required, then full physical assistance would be employed at the initiation of instruction because it would generally be considered most directive. This is a very conservative approach to prompt selection; however, data collected during instructional sessions should quickly reveal whether movement to a less directive level of assistance is appropriate.

A Few Words About Verbal Prompts

In practice, teachers frequently pair verbal with other types of prompts even though the student does not initially respond to the verbal prompt alone. It might be found, for example, that the student will insert his or her arm in a coat sleeve given partial physical assistance, but will not perform the behavior when told, "Put your arm in the sleeve," or some similar cue. Even when verbal direction has been found ineffective in evoking the response, we have observed that many teachers may nonetheless provide it concurrent with the presentation of the effective prompt (e.g., partial physical assistance).

As a general rule, we strongly recommend against such a practice. If a prompt is ineffective, pairing it with an effective prompt will not make the ineffective prompt more effective. A much more likely outcome of the pairing process is that the ineffective prompt will acquire control over the response and will then become one more aspect of instruction that must be faded out prior to the achievement of independent performance. In other words, you may build in an extra (and unnecessary) step in transferring control of the response from artificial to natural cues. In most cases, the fewer instructional prompts, the better.

There is, however, an exception to the general rule. That exception involves instances in which you want to build the controlling power of some verbal cue. For example, some response forms included in a routine may be of value in many contexts; this is particularly true of communication forms. It may, therefore, be useful to build the effectiveness of a single, easily administered verbal prompt that can then be used to teach the student to employ the behavior in a variety of situations. Such a case may be observed on the 1st, 6th, and 11th steps of Gary's Bus to Classroom routine.

On each of the steps specified as a communication target, the intent was to teach Gary to ask for help when needed. This skill is one that would be useful in many situations. Because the teacher felt it would be most efficient to use a verbal prompt to teach Gary the appropriate occasions for skill use in the future, she specified that a verbal prompt would be paired with the effective prompt (full physical assistance) during instruction. She wanted to develop the power of the verbal direction as a controlling stimulus so that she could use it, rather than physical assistance, to teach Gary those circumstances under which he should request help.

In exceptions such as the above, it is recommended that prompt fading during instruction be accomplished by first eliminating the initially effective prompt. Fading procedures may then be applied to the prompt that has (hopefully) acquired controlling properties. Examples of that process are included in Gary's Instructional Data Sheet (Figure 9.3 and 9.5–9.7, Step 1) to be discussed later in the chapter under "Decision Rules Applied" (see Step 1, page 90).

Positive Consequences During Assessment

During assessment, positive consequences may occasionally be delivered following performance of steps and/or routines in order to motivate participation from the student. Such consequences should be based on reinforcement inventory results (see the "What Does Your Child/Student Like" section of inventories) and should approximate those available in natural environments as closely as possible. Do not, for example, employ food as as a consequence if social rewards such as praise, a pat on the back, or eye contact and a smile are likely to act as reinforcers.

INSTRUCTIONAL PROCEDURES

Using and Fading Assistance

During instruction, teacher assistance is used to ensure that students achieve the critical effect of routines with as few errors as possible. In fact, the most important outcome of the assessment process was to determine the specific nature of prompts that would result in correct responding on each step of the routine. Instruction, then, begins with the teacher providing the appropriate type of assistance for each step in turn. Because such assistance will not generally be available to prompt responding in nontraining environments, it must be faded. The desired result of the fading process is skill performance by the student in the presence of appropriate, natural cues. To achieve that effect, we employ a technique that combines *decreasing assistance* and *time delay* fading methods (Billingsley & Romer, 1983; Wolery & Gast, 1984).

As previously noted, instruction begins with the type of assistance selected during the assessment process. The amount of assistance is then gradually reduced until the student performs the skill independently in the presence of natural cues. That reduction requires the teacher to identify one or two (or sometimes more) levels of assistance of the same general type used in initial instruction and that are intermediate between the initial prompt type and independence. Those intermediate levels, which may be determined during the course of instruction, are then described directly on the Instructional Data Sheet (Figure 9.2).

In the Bus to Classroom routine, assessment on the eighth step suggested the use of partial physical assistance for "walks to classroom." An intermediate level of prompt could be a touch on the arm that does not guide the movement, but serves to evoke the response. On the second step, assessment indicated that Gary would walk down the aisle of the bus following the directive verbal cue, "Go to class." Additional verbal prompts that (presumably) provide lesser degrees of direction could then be identified and employed by the teacher. In Gary's example, such prompts could include the questions, "Where do you go now" and/or "What's next?"

Until the student meets the criterion for movement to the independent level of responding, all artificial prompts employed in instructional sessions are provided immediately following the natural cue. That is, the teacher does not give the student the opportunity to make an error by waiting to see if the student responds on his or her own. Returning to the Bus to Classroom example, the teacher would provide the appropriate type and level of assistance to prompt walking to the classroom as soon as Gary entered the school building rather than waiting to determine whether he would respond unassisted.

As instruction proceeds, the student receives less and less assistance, with the speed of fading being dependent on his or her performance. When the student meets the criterion for movement to independence on any step, he or she is then given the opportunity to respond without an artificial prompt. If he or she does not begin to respond within the allowable latency in the presence of the natural cue, the teacher provides *full physical assistance* to maximize the probability that the student will perform the step successfully without making additional errors. For the same reason, full physical assistance is recommended on any step (regardless of type of instructional prompt being used) if the student begins to make an incorrect response or fails to start his or her response within the latency period.

Although our own observations and the work of others (Horner, 1988) indicate that providing a degree of assistance that will ensure success often acts to reduce aggressive behaviors, it is possible that full physical assistance following failures to respond will provoke aggression by some students. In those cases, it is recommended that the least amount of assistance that produced the desired response in the past be provided and that additional increases in assistance be employed if failures to respond continue. If the teacher arrives at a point at which full physical assistance is once again required and aggression results, a brief period of time-out may be applied, following which the routine should be started from the beginning. Should full physical assistance continue to evoke aggression in sessions that follow, the possible communicative intent of the behavior should be examined and the problem dealt with as discussed in Chapter 11, "Behavior Problems: A Special Form of Communication."

Use of Reinforcers and Massed Practice

The underlying philosophy of the IMPACT instructional paradigm is that students will learn and use those skills that have allowed them to successfully and efficiently achieve critical effects. It is also presumed that the presentation of instructional trials distributed across those times and circumstances in which the skill would naturally be of value facilitates skill acquisition (cf. Bambara, Warren, & Komisar, 1988; Kayser, Billingsley, & Neel, 1985). The emphasis of instruction, then, is on providing, and then fading, the assistance required for successful achievement of critical effects. Generally, positive consequences other than the routine's critical effect should be limited to social praise. In addition, such praise should approximate the type and frequency that would likely be available in nontraining environments.

If successful completion of the routine accompanied by natural levels of social praise is sufficient to promote adequate progress by the student, do not use any additional training reinforcers. If they are not required, they simply become one more element of instruction that must be faded out due to their unavailability in nontraining situations.

Occasionally, manipulations of prompts may fail to result in adequate performance on some steps of a routine. In those cases, it may be necessary to introduce training reinforcers or provide natural reinforcers on unnatural schedules (i.e., more or less frequently than they would normally occur). Persistent duration errors, for example, may often be reduced by changing amounts, types, or density of reinforcers. It might also be appropriate to modify typical IMPACT procedures by using massed practice. For example, continued errors in the actual form of the response could indicate that the student needs more opportunities for practice. In that case, it might be effective to implement several practice trials in a row for the particular problem step, perhaps accompanied by artificial reinforcers to maintain responding within a massed trial format.

Should you elect to use training reinforcers, then information derived from the environmental inventories, your own informal observations, or structured assessments in which paired choices from a group of potential reinforcers are offered and then prioritized on the basis of student responses (Pelland & Falvey, 1986) can help you choose appropriate consequences. In all cases, however, keep in mind that reinforcers that the child will not receive outside of the training situation (i.e., are not part of the natural critical effect) should be faded. Otherwise, maintenance of performance in nontraining settings is highly unlikely.

If massed practice is selected as an instructional intervention, data collection procedures and decision rules developed specifically for that instructional format may be followed (e.g., White, 1985). When using this type of intervention, it is important to remember that the criterion for success is correct responding within the routine;

therefore, an opportunity to evaluate the response as part of the routine during instructional sessions must still be provided.

CHANGING THE PROGRAM

The decision to move from one level of assistance to another, or to make other program changes, should be based upon student perfomance data. Procedures for measuring performance and guidelines for making instructional changes are the topics of the following sections.

Measuring Performance

Performance during instructional sessions is assessed in blocks of three consecutive trials. The student performs the routine on three occasions at appropriate, naturally occurring times. Each trial constitutes one complete instructional session, and the number of sessions per day is limited only by the number of natural opportunities available for skill performance. Some routines may occur several times per day while others may occur less than once every day. The total time it takes to assess performance on three consecutive trials, therefore, will vary from routine to routine. Sessions should follow program guidelines as outlined in the Instructional Conditions and Comments form (Figure 9.4) on the back of the Instructional Data Sheet illustrated in Figure 9.3. Information to be provided on that form includes the behavioral objective, program manager(s), and appropriate times and situations ("Conditions") for training. Space is also available for any comments or special instructions you may wish to include as the program progresses.

Instruction begins with the student being given the required level of assistance for each step as determined by the assessment. Correct or error responses are recorded on the Instructional Data Sheet for each step and consequences are provided accordingly. Two types of errors should be recorded: 1) latency error (EL): the student did not begin to respond to the cue before the end of the allowable latency period, and 2) response error (E): the form of the response was incorrect. A response error (E), for example, might be recorded for the "walks to building entry" step of the Bus to Classroom routine if Gary ran (or attempted to run) across the lawn and through the bushes rather than walking to the building on the sidewalk.

A third error type could also be of concern in routines. This is a duration error (ED). Duration errors were noted infrequently for pupils with autism participating in field tests of the IMPACT curriculum. Such errors may be recorded, however, if duration problems were noted for a step during initial assessment sessions or in probe sessions (which are discussed on page 93 of this chapter). Duration errors may be indicated on the Instructional Data Sheet by circling the time in the duration column, in addition to noting ED.

A duration error consists of a prompted or independent correct response form that is initiated within the specified latency, but that takes longer for the pupil to complete than the maximum allowed duration. It was found during assessment, for example, that Gary began to "take off coat" independently within the 3-second latency, but exceeded the allotted time of 7 seconds to complete the response. Duration of step performance, therefore, was timed during instructional sessions and duration errors recorded. If, during instruction, three consecutive correct responses are com-

Instructional Data Sheet

Manager: _____ Helen _____

Name: _____ Gary _____
Routine: _____ Bus to classroom _____
Date: _____

Beginning natural cue: _____ Teacher approaches Gary _____
Critical effect: _____ Participation in classroom activities _____
Latency: _____ 3 seconds _____   Duration of routine: _____ 3'10" _____

FIGURE 9.3

Duration	Step	Assistance	Date	Date	Date	Assistance	Date	Date	Date
2 sec	1. Requests help with seatbelt ©	Say "Show me 'help.'" Mold sign for "help."	C	C	C	/ Continue verbal cue, slightly lift / hand.	C	E	C
15 sec	2. Walks down aisle	"Go to class."	EL	C	C		C	C	C
10 sec	3. Picks up lunch box or other materials	I	C	C	C		C	C	E
5 sec	4. Exits bus	I	C	C	EL		EL	EL	C
35 sec	5. Walks to building entry	Hold his hand while walking	C	E	C		E	E	E
2 sec	6. Requests help with door ©	Say "Show me 'help.'" Mold sign for "help."	C	C	C	/ Continue verbal cue, slightly lift / hand.	E	C	C
2 sec	7. Enters building	Hold his hand while entering building	C	C	C	/ Touch on hand.	EL	C	C
60 sec	8. Walks to classroom	Hold his hand while walking	E	C	C		C	C	C
10 sec	9. Puts away lunch box and other materials	Take his hands and guide to shelf	C	C	C	/ Guide ½ way to shelf	C	C	C
(7 sec)	10. Takes off coat	I	ED	EL ED	ED	Set timer for 7 sec. If Gary beats timer, / / give praise & "high five." (See note 1.)	C	ED	C
2 sec	11. Requests help finding hook ©	Say "Show me 'help.'" Mold sign for "help."	C	C	C	/ Continue verbal cue, slightly lift / hand.	C	C	C
4 sec	12. Hangs up coat	Point at hook	C	C	EL		C	C	C
	Total duration:								

EL = Latency error
E = Response form error
ED = Duration error
C = Correct

© = Communication target

Program changes:
/ = Change in assistance
// = Change in consequence

83

FIGURE 9.4

Instructional Conditions and Comments

Objective

Gary will walk from the bus to the classroom upon arrival at school within 3'10" by (date). Assistance will not be given unless Gary signs "help" independently (see task analysis). Success judged by Ms. Lawrence. Gary will also walk from the bus to his home after school requesting "help" as needed when accompanied by a parent.

Success judged from parental report.

Manager (parent, teacher, other supervisory individual)

Helen

Conditions (appropriate times and situations)

Instruction occurs when bus arrives at loading/unloading area, approximately 8:00 a.m. The program will be conducted by Ms. Lawrence or Mr. Bernard on basis of availability.

Comments, special instructions

Note 1, (date). Gary seems to have all the moves down, but gets distracted easily by things going on in and outside of the classroom. Decided to use a Beat the Clock game rather than giving him more assistance. If he beats the clock, give descriptive praise and "high five."

Note 2, (date). Continue to keep track of time with watch, but don't use obvious kitchen timer. Continue enthusiastic, descriptive praise.

Note 3, (date). G. signed "help" before I could ask him what he wanted. From now on, signing should be independent.

Note 4, (date). G. found coat hook on his own—no help needed! Discontinue signing for help on this step. G. should find his hook independently.

pleted within the desired duration, timing of step performance may be terminated in future instructional sessions. Additional checks on duration will be conducted within probe sessions.

Recording Data

Correct and error data are recorded on the Instructional Data Sheet; program changes are indicated on this sheet by slash marks (/ or //) as included in the data sheet examples. Where a level of assistance change occurs, follow a *single* slash mark with a brief description of the new prompt in the space provided. If reinforcer or other program changes are implemented, use a *double* slash mark as an indicator and briefly indicate the nature of the change. It is recommended that, as the program progresses, Short Forms of the Instructional Data Sheet as illustrated in Figures 9.5, 9.6, 9.7 be overlayed on the original sheet to avoid having to recopy routine task analysis information following every six trials.

GUIDELINES FOR INSTRUCTIONAL CHANGES

Data-based rules for modifying programs described in this section are intended to provide a framework for instructional decision-making. They are not meant to prevent you from developing your own rules based on experience with particular students, nor do they cover all possible instructional options. Successful program outcomes, however, have resulted from the implementation of similar practices during field tests of, and research based on, the IMPACT Curriculum (Donnellan & Neel, 1986; Kayser et al., 1986; Neel, Billingsley, & Lambert, 1983).

The rules are to be applied to each step within a routine. The sequence of rules is designed to ensure that instructional procedures will not be continued indefinitely if the student does not progress and that teacher assistance, and/or artificial consequences, will be withdrawn on the basis of student capability.

Making Decisions

IMPACT decision rules are illustrated in the Figure 9.8 flowchart. Details regarding their use are as follows:

I. Begin by collecting data on three instructional trials and record correct and error responses on the Instructional Data Sheet. As previously noted, a trial is one complete movement through a given routine. Of course, the more frequently data are collected, the more timely will be your instructional decisions. Under ideal circumstances, then, data should be collected on each instructional trial. If it is not possible to assess student performance on such a frequent schedule, it is recommended that data be collected on at least every other trial.

After performance has been assessed on three trials, count the number correct. That is, count the number of trials on which the student exhibited the correct response with the prescribed amount of teacher assistance within the allowable latency (and, perhaps, within the allotted duration). Generally, the rules will be used to help you decide when to increase or decrease the amount of as-

Instructional Data Sheet (Short Form)

FIGURE 9.5

Page #: 2
Name: Gary

Routine: Bus to classroom
Latency: 3 seconds

Assistance	Date	Date	Date	Assistance	Date	Date	Date	Date
Continue verbal cue; slightly lift hand.	C	C	C	/ Verbal cue only	E	EL	EL	
/ Ask "What's next?"	C	C	C	/ I	C	EL	C	
I	EL	C	C	I	C	C	C	
/ Say "Go."	C	C	C	/ I	C	C	C	
/ Guide Gary rather than just hold / hand.	E	C	E	/ Guide; if Gary resists or breaks / away, start step over.	E	E	C	
Continue verbal cue; slightly lift hand.	C	C	C	/ Verbal cue only	C	EL	C	
Touch on hand.	C	C	C	/ I	EL	C	C	
/ Constant touch on arm.	C	C	C	/ Touch on arm ³/₄ way to classroom.	C	E	C	
Use light touch with fingers to / guide ¹/₂ way.	EL	C	EL	Use firmer touch at beginning of / movement.	C	C	C	
Set timer for 1 sec. If Gary beats timer, give praise & "high five."	C	C	C	Drop "high five!" Continue praise / & timer.	C	C	C	
/ Verbal cue only.	C	EL	C		C	C	C	
/ Nod head toward hook.	EL	C	C		C	C	C	

Total duration: 3'30"

Cut along dotted line.

Instructional Data Sheet (Short Form)

FIGURE 9.6

Page #: 3

Name: Gary

Routine: Bus to classroom

Latency: 3 seconds

Assistance	Date	Date	Date
Continue verbal cue; tap hand upward	C	C	C
I	C	C	C
I	C	C	C
Guide; if Gary resists or breaks away, start step over.	C	C	C
Verbal cue only.	C	C	C
I	E	C	E
Touch on arm 3/4 way to classroom.	C	C	C
/ Light touch to guide 1/2 way.	C	EL	C
// Praise only (note 2)	ED	C	C
/ Ask "What do you want?"	EL	C	C
/ I	C	C	C

Assistance	Date	Date	Date
/ Verbal cue only	C	C	EL
	C	EL	C
	C	C	C
// Guide only.	C	C	C
/ Ask "What do you want?"	C	C	EL
/ Lighter touch on hand.	C	C	C
/ Touch on arm 1/2 way to classroom.	C	C	C
	C	C	C
	C	C	C
	C	C	C
	C	C	C

Total duration:

Instructional Data Sheet (Short Form)

FIGURE 9.7

Page #: 4
Name: Gary

Routine: Bus to classroom
Latency: 3 seconds

Assistance	Date	Date	Date	Assistance	Date	Date	Date
Verbal cue only.	C	C	C	/ Ask "What do you want?"	C	C	C / I (see note 3.)
I	C	C	EL		EL	C	C
I	C	EL	C		C	C	C
I	C	C	C		C	C	C
/ Hold hand, but don't guide!	C	C	C	/ Hold hand ½ way to building	C	E	C
Ask "What do you want?"	C	C	C	/ I	C	C	C
/ I	C	C	C		C	C	C
/ Touch on arm ¼ way to classroom.	E	E	E	/ Touch on arm first ¼ way to classroom plus lighter touch past Mr. Raymond's room.	C	C	C
/ I	EL	E	EL	/ Tap on hand.	C	EL	EL
/ / Reduce praise to "Good."	C	C	ED		C	EL	C
/ I New target: Find hook.	Found hook. Note 4. / I	C	C		C	C	C
I	C	C	C		C	C	C

Total duration: 3'08"

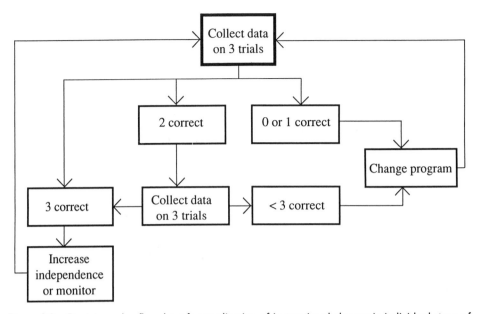

Figure 9.8. Decision rules flowchart for application of instructional change in individual steps of routines.

sistance provided in the form of prompts. If, however, the rules are used to guide decisions concerning consequences, it is recommended that two blocks of three trials be administered when new consequences are added and that decisions be based on responding within the second block. This procedure is suggested in order to permit the student a reasonable number of opportunities to sample new contingencies.

A. If all three trials are scored as correct, move to greater independence and return to I above.

Comment. Greater independence on the part of the student could be achieved by changing the level of prompt (i.e., fading the prompt) or, if prompts have been faded, by fading any artificial reinforcers. If both prompts and reinforcers have been faded, movement to greater independence is, of course, impossible. Continue to monitor performance on those steps and, if it is not likely that a manager (e.g., parent or other supervisory individual) will be present in nontraining situations when the behavior should occur, begin to fade your presence. This may be accomplished, for instance, by increasing your distance from the student and/or increasing the frequency with which you conceal yourself from his or her view. If you cannot easily collect appropriate data under such circumstances, information supplied by informants, such as other teachers, aides, secretarial staff, other students, or community members can frequently tell you what you need to know concerning the adequacy of the student's performance.

A possible option for continued instruction on some steps might be to implement procedures to increase the sophistication of the response form. If, for example, a student has learned to eat with adapted utensils, further instruction might focus on the use of regular silverware.

B. If fewer than two trials are scored as correct, change the program and return to I above.

Comment.   Most changes made because the student is not progressing at an adequate pace will be those requiring the use of a new prompt that increases the amount of teacher assistance. The *type* of prompt (e.g., verbal, gestural, physical) should, in most cases, remain the same, but the extent to which it is likely to provide information to the student should be increased. For example, if a gestural prompt from across the room was successful in producing a "go to the sink" response on fewer than two trials, the teacher could position himself or herself in proximity to the sink and point to it. If the assessed prompt of partial physical assistance (see Figure 9.2) was found to be inadequate, the teacher might guide the student further in the direction of the sink.

It is recommended that the teacher employ a change involving consequences only after trying at least two changes in degree of assistance without success. An exception, however, could be those cases in which the student does not perform the response with adequate speed, but obviously possesses the skills necessary to perform the response fluently. An example of such a situation is provided in the illustration of application of the decision rules (see the next section below).

Where consequences are modified, changes could involve manipulations of type, amount, or schedule. Frequently, training reinforcers are introduced to influence the speed with which the student performs a step. In those cases, the nature of the change often requires that the student complete the step within the allotted time interval in order to receive the reinforcer.

    C.   If two responses are scored as correct, go to II.

II.   Collect data on three instructional trials.

    A.   If three responses are scored as correct, move to greater independence according to IA.

    B.   If not, change the program and return to I.

    Comment.   If the student gives a spontaneous independent response before the prompt can be provided at any point in the preceding sequence, the criterion for a correct response should immediately be changed to independent functioning.

III.   When independent performance has been achieved on all steps, time performance of the entire routine. If performance time is satisfactory, conduct generalization probes and, if successful generalization is achieved, implement the maintenance probe schedule. If performance time is not satisfactory, conduct additional training to improve fluency.

Decision Rules Applied

To give you a better feel for the use of the rules in practice, Gary's progress and the instructional procedures used by his teacher on a few of the steps of his Bus to Classroom routine are outlined below. As indicated on the Instructional Conditions and Comments form (Figure 9.4), the program was conducted once each day at 8:00 a.m. with either the teacher or her aide acting as program manager.

Step 1.   The first step, "Requests help with seatbelt," is a communication target. Assessment indicated that Gary needed full physical assistance to perform that step. As noted previously, however, his teacher wanted to build the controlling power of the verbal cue, "Show me 'help'," and, therefore, decided to pair that cue with the physical assistance she provided.

The first three days of data (Figure 9.3) show that Gary signed "Help" correctly and within the desired latency when cued verbally and molded to do so. The decision specified by the rules, then, is to move to greater independence. The teacher accomplished that change by continuing to provide the verbal cue, but only lifting Gary's hand slightly rather than completely molding the sign.

On the next three days, Gary scored two correct responses and one error. In such a case, the rules suggest collecting data on three more trials. On those trials (Figure 9.5), Gary performed correctly each time. He was, therefore, again moved to greater independence by the teacher, who omitted all physical prompts.

Following removal of physical assistance, Gary made errors on each trial. The rules indicate that if fewer than two trials are scored as correct, the program should be changed to increase the probability of correct responding. The teacher decided to reintroduce physical prompts, but to give less assistance than such prompts had previously provided. The program change, then, was to continue the verbal cue, but to pair it with an upward tap on Gary's hand. Figure 9.6 data indicate that the program change was successful and that Gary responded correctly on each of the three trials that followed.

On the basis of the three correct responses, Gary's teacher once again removed the physical prompt, but continued the verbal cue. This resulted in two correct responses and one latency error on the next three trials. The rules specify that a second block of three trials be administered in such a case and, when those trials were conducted, Gary scored correct on each occasion (Figure 9.7).

Having successfully faded her physical assistance, the teacher now began to fade the verbal cue. As indicated in Figure 9.7, she decided to only ask Gary, "What do you want?" On the first trial, Gary responded correctly. On the second trial, he signed "help" before the teacher had the opportunity to provide the prompt. When such an anticipation occurs, it is recommended that the teacher move immediately to the independent level on subsequent trials. Gary's teacher followed that recommendation and indicated the requirement for independent performance on the Instructional Data Sheet and explained the circumstances in Note 3 of the Instructional Conditions and Comments form (Figure 9.4) on the reverse side of the Instructional Data Sheet. From then on, the teacher could simply monitor Gary's performance on that step to ensure that he maintained his independent performance. Of course, she may decide to change the instructional target in the near future to teach Gary to undo his own seatbelt. (See Step 11, "Requests help finding hook," for an example of that type of change.)

Step 5. The fifth step of the routine is to teach Gary to walk to the building entrance independently after he leaves the bus. Based on assessment information, instruction began with the teacher providing partial physical assistance; that is, she held his hand while walking to the entrance, but did not directly guide his movements. On the first three trials, Figure 9.3 data indicate that Gary responded correctly twice. Once, however, he broke away from the teacher and had to be physically moved back onto the walkway. Since he had made two correct responses, the teacher provided another block of three trials as recommended by the decision rules.

Unfortunately, on the second block of trials, he broke away on all three occasions. Since fewer than three responses were scored as correct (in fact, they were *all* errors), a program change was indicated. The teacher decided to guide Gary from the bus to the school entrance rather than simply holding his hand and collected three more days of data (see Figure 9.5). Once again, the rules indicated a program change because Gary scored fewer than two correct responses.

We have noted that, in most instances, at least two levels of assistance changes should be made before manipulating consequences. In this case, however, the teacher was providing about as much assistance as she could; she was giving full physical assistance all the way to the entrance of the school building. She therefore added a consequence (note the double slash marks on the Instructional Data Sheet [Figure 9.6]) for error responses. The consequence was that if Gary resisted walking to the building or broke away, they started the step over again; that is, Gary was guided back to the bus exit and they once again began walking toward the building entry. The result of that intervention during the first block of three trials was that Gary made only one correct response. In accordance with guidelines associated with the rules, however, the program was not changed following that block of trials, in order to give Gary several opportunities to experience the new consequence. Three more trials were then provided using the same procedure.

As noted in Figure 9.6, Gary performed all three trials correctly. In accordance with the rules, the teacher moved him toward greater independence by removing the consequences, but maintaining the guidance. That change also resulted in three correct trials.

Since three trials were performed with success, the decision rules indicate that additional movement should be provided toward independence. The teacher therefore reimplemented her initial type of assistance (i.e., holding his hand, but not directing) and assessed performance on three more trials (Figure 9.7). As all responses were again correct, assistance was reduced further, with the teacher holding Gary's hand only half way to the classroom.

With the reduction in assistance described above, Gary performed two out of the three trials without error. No intervention need be made at this point, however. Rather, data from three more trials should be collected before the teacher determines to continue to fade assistance or whether to make some remedial change to promote correct responding on a more consistent basis.

Step 10. By circling the duration allotted for performance on the Instructional Data Sheet (Figure 9.3), the teacher has indicated that Gary took longer than 7 seconds to take off his coat during assessment, even though he was able to perform the skill independently. Duration errors, therefore, must be recorded during instruction until Gary takes off his coat within the time limit on three consecutive trials.

On the first block of trials, Gary made three duration errors and, on one trial, also made a latency error. Since he achieved fewer than two correct responses, the decision rules recommend a change of program. The teacher had observed that Gary seemed to know quite well all of the movements that were involved in taking his coat off, but just dawdled in doing so. He particularly liked to look around the room to see what the teachers and other students were doing and to observe the activity in the courtyard through the classroom window. The teacher, therefore, implemented a change in consequences designed to increase Gary's performance speed.

The teacher explained to Gary that they were going to have a contest in which he should try to beat the clock. As indicated in Figure 9.3, the intervention involved setting a timer for 7 seconds as soon as Gary put away his lunchbox. If he had his coat off before the timer bell rang, the teacher praised him for his rapid performance and gave him a "high five" hand shake.

As noted in Figure 9.5, Gary took his coat off without any duration errors during the second block of three trials following the "beat the clock" procedure. She therefore moved him toward greater independence by dropping the "high five," but continuing the timer and praise.

Because Gary made three correct responses with only the timer and praise, the teacher then stopped using the timer (Figure 9.6). For the next three trials, Gary made one error response and two correct responses. Consistent with the decision rules, data were collected for three more days and it was found that Gary consistently removed his coat with adequate speed.

Based on his consistent, correct, fluent responding, the teacher's next change was to continue to fade the consequence by reducing the praise to the single comment, "Good," if Gary's coat was off in time (Figure 9.7). Two out of three responses were then performed satisfactorily, so no change was made. On the next block of trials, Gary removed his coat within the allotted time period and independently on each of the trials. Although not illustrated in this example, the next logical step would be to see if the praise could be completely faded without an accompanying decrease in speed of performance. Since the teacher has taken care to fade the consequences systematically and slowly, chances look good!

PROBES

Various types of probe assessments are conducted during training and at various times following skill acquisition. This section describes the purpose and nature of each type of probe.

Probes should be conducted at least once a month to assess maintenance of previously learned skills and once every two weeks to observe progress that may have gone undetected on skills currently under instruction. In addition, probes should be conducted following skill acquisition to assess generalization to nontraining environments. Probes, therefore, are of three types: *independence probes, generalization probes,* and *maintenance probes.*

Maintenance and independence probe sessions are very similar to initial assessment sessions (see *Assessment Procedures,* page 74). They are, however, conducted only once rather than three or more times. Performance on each step should be recorded as during initial assessment, but duration of each step need not be recorded when maintenance probes are conducted, except as explained below.

Independence Probes

Independence probes are conducted for routines currently under instruction and are intended primarily to determine whether the pupil has acquired greater independence in the performance of routine steps than our instructional and evaluation practices have allowed us to observe. These probes, however, will also indicate whether duration problems have developed for steps previously performed with adequate fluency. It was previously suggested that independence probes be conducted every two weeks. In terms of the logistics of instructional decision-making, you will probably find it easiest to conduct these probes at the end of a three-session cycle for any given routine.

1.   If independent performance is noted during the probe session on any step for which assistance is being delivered during instructional sessions, move the pupil to independent responding on that step. When unanticipated independence is noted during the probe, it is quite possible that the step-by-step guidelines for fading assistance have actually prevented the pupil from demonstrating progress.

2.   For the same reasons noted in 1 above, change the level of assistance used during instructional sessions if a lesser level of assistance is recorded during the probe session.

3.   If a duration problem is noted for any step during the probe session, duration of step performance should be timed in instructional sessions and duration errors recorded. Follow procedures as outlined in the "Measuring Performance" section of this chapter (page 82).

Generalization Probes

Once data indicate that the student has acquired a skill at the specified level of independence in the training setting(s) you have selected, it is essential that probes be conducted to assess whether skill generalization has been achieved. The point of such probes is to determine whether the student will perform the routine in appropriate, *untrained* situations in the presence of individuals other than the teacher. Generalization probes are an integral part of the data collection system and provide the ultimate test of instructional success.

Often, generalization probes are most appropriately administered by parents because they are frequently the student's primary caregiver. When parents conduct generalization probes, it is usually unreasonable to ask them to collect data in the same way you do. Rather, it will probably be most productive to ask them to observe the student on a few occasions when skill performance is naturally required and let you know whether the their child's performance was satisfactory. During such probes, parents should be advised not to use special assistance or consequences. Of course, natural cues and consequences are acceptable. Remember, you are interested in how well the student performs under normal, nontraining conditions. (See White [1988] for a comprehensive set of guidelines for conducting generalization probes.)

If performance is satisfactory, your instructional program has been successful. However, if caregivers are not satisfied with student performance, you must ask about the specific problems that caused the dissatisfaction and then redesign instruction to include strategies to facilitate generalization.

The generalization probes outlined in this section are a formal way for you to assess performance in untrained situations. Informally, however, parents should be encouraged to be alert for the spontaneous performance of target skills as training progresses and ensure that the student achieves critical effects associated with those skills. If satisfactory skill performance occurs in specified nontraining situations before instruction is concluded, you may, of course, terminate instruction on that routine and implement a maintenance probe schedule.

Maintenance Probes

Maintenance probes are undertaken on all routines learned during the academic year that the pupil can perform: 1) at the lowest selected level of assistance, 2) with the most natural consequences and 3) within an acceptable duration. If response form errors are observed during maintenance checks, remedial steps should be implemented. It might be found, for example, that a student no longer uses a trained gesture to indicate that he or she needs help, but rather screams to achieve the communicative function. One potential method to decrease the screams and increase gesturing might be to retrain appropriate persons so that they would be more attentive to, or even prompt, the gesture and ignore the screams.

In addition to noting response form errors, the total duration of the routines should be timed during maintenance checks. If the routine is not performed within the maximum allowable duration, additional checks should be conducted to identify specific routine steps that require more fluent performance, and instruction should be conducted to increase fluency.

Of course, whenever any routine is placed on a maintenance schedule, a new routine should be added for instruction. The pupil should continually be provided with the opportunity to increase his or her repertoire of functional skills.

Avoiding and Remediating Generalization and Maintenance Problems

The avoidance and remediation of generalization and maintenance problems have been discussed in considerable detail in works such as Haring (1988); Horner (1988); Stokes and Baer (1977); and Wolery, Bailey, and Sugai (1988). The following recommendations are based on those works, as well as our own observations, and appear critical to skill performance across time and across a variety of natural situations in which training has not been conducted.

1.   At least four characteristics of the IMPACT curriculum development and instructional process should contribute substantially to generalized and maintained responding. First, skills targeted for instruction should be those that are reinforced in natural environments; that is, they allow the student to achieve critical effects. Second, because skill selection is based on an inventory of behaviors actually needed within those environments in which the student must function, skills taught will usually be those that are used frequently and in several situations. Third, skills are learned within natural contexts and in the presence of natural cues. Fourth, students are taught to perform skills fluently; that is, at a rate that ensures efficient access to the critical effect. Because each of the preceding curriculum characteristics is important to generalization and/or maintenance, you should double check target skills, the instructional plan, and mastery criteria prior to instruction to ensure consistency with those characteristics.

2.   Instruction will usually have little value unless the skills that are taught occur in natural, untrained situations. Unfortunately, goals and objectives written for students with moderate to severe handicaps often imply that students will be taught to perform a behavior only within a single, training context. If generalization is, in fact, a desired outcome, behavioral goals and objectives should specify the nature of generalized performance. Explicit statements of criteria for generalization should facilitate both the evaluation of generalized outcomes and the selection of appropriate instructional practices (Billingsley, 1984; Billingsley, 1988). At the very least, such statements should act as reminders to those in charge of instructional programs that training has not been completed until the student can perform target skills in the real world.

3.   As you teach, vary stimuli and situations. Where a skill needs to be performed in several different situations (e.g., fast food restaurants, grocery stores, parks) and/or

with a variety of materials (e.g., sweaters, vending machines, price indicators, radios), it is important that examples used in instruction are representative of those situations or materials. Similarly, the student must learn those situations in which skill performance is not appropriate and, therefore, must be withheld (e.g., undressing to change into a swimming suit is acceptable in the pool dressing room, but not on the bus on the way to the pool). Learning when to withhold a response also requires that situations or stimuli be varied so that the student encounters conditions under which a behavior is inappropriate. When you reinforce instances of appropriate performance, and withholding reinforcement for inappropriate responses, students can learn to discriminate appropriate from inappropriate occasions for skill performance. Horner, McDonnell, and Bellamy (1986) have provided detailed guidelines for varying stimuli in instructional programs within both community and simulation settings.

4. Attempt to minimize chances that the student will be able to achieve the critical effect without performing the target behavior. For example, you might teach a student to engage in socially appropriate forms of conversation rather than echolalia or bizarre comments. One of the critical effects of socially appropriate conversation should be the sustained attention of the listener. If the student finds he or she can achieve that effect in nontraining environments without using the newly taught forms, the probability of generalization and maintenance will be greatly reduced. Implementing this principle may call for modifications within natural environments. Significant persons in the student's home and community (e.g., parents, peers, staff of the local convenience food store) may have to be reminded that it is crucial for the student to be permitted to achieve the critical effect only upon exhibiting the target skill, not when producing some less desirable response form or doing nothing. Some tactful, low key training may even be necessary.

5. Make sure that either the critical effect that the pupil achieves in the training setting is available in nontraining settings or that the routine results in a functionally equivalent outcome. A student who washes the dishes in a training situation might be permitted to participate immediately in some highly valued activity upon completion, perhaps free time to play with a favorite toy or instruction in vending machine operation that leads to receipt of a soft drink or candy bar. At home, washing the dishes might result in parental praise and the opportunity to watch television. If neither of those outcomes represents a critical effect for the student, it is likely that the dishwashing behavior will not be maintained for an extended period of time. The teacher must then either work with the parents to identify effects available in the home that are as powerful as those used in training or instructional steps must be implemented to increase the power of the praise and television consequences that the parents normally provide. For example, praise following dishwashing could be paired with toy play. This is essentially the process of developing secondary reinforcers.

SUMMARY

In this chapter, we have attempted to describe an integrated set of instructional procedures in considerable detail. In fact, so much detail may have been included that those procedures seem considerably more complex than they actually are. The direct relationship of one element of the process to the next should contribute to effective and efficient application in practical situations. However, because the relationship between elements may tend to get lost across pages of text, the following list provides a summary of critical IMPACT instructional steps:

1. Task analyze the routine.
2. Perform a dry run of the analysis.
    A. Modify the analysis as necessary on the basis of the dry run.
3. Assess student performance on each step of the routine.
4. Select appropriate types of assistance for initial instruction.
5. Implement instruction of the routine within a natural context (i.e., a natural time and reason should exist for performing the routine).
6. Collect data on performance of each step.
7. Apply rules for program change.
    A. Fade assistance or other training procedures if student is making satisfactory progress.
    B. Increase assistance or introduce/change other training procedures if progress is not satisfactory.
8. Obtain independent, fluent performance of routine.
9. Conduct independence probes on a biweekly schedule and change the program as indicated.
10. Conduct generalization probes and implement remedial instruction if generalization is not achieved, and return to 5.
11. Implement maintenance probe schedule if generalization is achieved.

10 > Teaching Communication in Context

This chapter highlights the importance of communication goals in the IMPACT instructional process. In Chapter 9 you learned about the instructional process. This chapter illustrates how you can integrate communication into each of your routines. By integrating communication instruction into each routine you will be effectively teaching communication throughout the whole school day. The opportunity to communicate exists in every interaction that takes place between two or more people. Providing training in these skills within a routine format means training a child in communication when and where it normally occurs. Instructing a child in communication in real situations, throughout a variety of daily routines, increases the probability that the child will learn when and where to use acquired skills. Any skill that a child can demonstrate during instructional sessions, but cannot use elsewhere, is not a functional skill, by definition. Communication skills that are functional in that they lead to a student's increased control over the environment are effective. By providing training in form and function in context, the problem of generalizing acquired skills across people and settings may be minimized. The goal of training functional communication skills is to enhance the ability of children with moderate to severe handicaps to be productive communicators. Training a child in skills when and where they normally occur within a natural social context should reduce the amount of instructional time needed for the child to become proficient in communication skills.

There are two distinct types of educational programming for teaching communication skills in routines. The first and most important is the type of routine you might use if you are trying to build additional functions. A sample of this type of routine is shown on page 103, "Communicating a Choice." The critical effect of the routine is to receive a chosen item or have access to a chosen activity. The purpose of the routine is to teach the child to get what he or she prefers by using a new communicative function. If the child successfully completes the routine, then he or she will have acquired another communicative function, that is, requesting needs and wants. What is distinctive about this kind of routine is that its goal is communication. Any routine that has as its outcome a communicative effort by the child is a communication routine. For a routine to be communicative, the child must express some kind of communicative intent. If you are using a communication routine, the routine itself must have a relevant context and must be a purposeful activity for the child.

Other times, communication targets may become an integral part of another routine. The communication program is taught by embedding communication forms within a variety of routines. This means that the critical effect of the routine may not be entirely communicative in nature but may include a transitional, recreation/leisure, community access, or self-help goal. A sample of this type of routine was provided in the Bus to Classroom example in Chapter 9 and is also provided in the Changing into School Clothes before Snack routine on page 103. The latter example has as its critical effect "going to snack" after changing gym clothes. Although the outcome of this routine is not communicative in nature, there are opportunities within the sequence of activities to target communication skills, in this case, signing "help." By including this communicative skill in a variety of routines, you can increase the number of available contexts to teach effective communication throughout the day. Teaching communication in this fashion is called "embedding communication skills."

Almost every routine will have some communication components. The difference between the two types illustrated here is one of degree. It is important to remember that, when you are developing your instructional plans, you must be sure to highlight as many opportunities as possible to teach the communication functions and forms that you have selected on your IMPACT Communication Form Selection Summary (page 67).

GUIDELINES FOR INSTRUCTION IN COMMUNICATION ROUTINES

The following guidelines are suggested for instruction in communication skills in a routine format at school, at home, and in the community.

1.   Identifying Relevant Contexts

For each communication skill that you will instruct, determine where and when the skill normally occurs. This can be accomplished by reviewing classroom routines and identifying several situations where the child can use the skill in context. This requires that you identify what outcome each skill should produce for the child (critical effect). If the goal is to communicate the desire to eat, using the skill should result in food for the child. You should teach the communication skills included in such a routine only where and when it is possible for the child to eat (i.e., lunch time or snack time). If the goal is to respond to the cue "What do you want?", you can teach this cue within a variety of routines whenever desirable items or activities are present. For instruction in choice skills, remember that, in order to keep the function of the skill intact, you will have to be prepared to follow through with each request. If you are unable to respond to the student's request, the communicative function of the request will probably not be understood by the student.

If you design a communication routine in which the end result is to teach a new communicative function, be sure that the sequence of activities also has relevant contexts. It must produce a critical effect for the child. The example, shown on page 103, of a communication routine for making a choice, has as its objective to teach the child how to request things that are not in his or her immediate environment. The sequence of events produces an immediate effect for the child, that is, whatever the child points to, he or she receives. This enables the child to learn the effect of the communication. Unless the item or activity is received, the only result of asking for something is praise for the effort. Undoubtedly, praise for making an effort is a good addition to many programs, but in this case it does not teach the communicative intent desired. Caution should be exercised when setting up communication routines to ensure that the *communicative intent* is realized through the desired *communication form*.

2. Facilitating Generalization

It is important to target as many different situations as possible for each communication skill you will be teaching. This will allow the child the opportunity to use each skill he or she learns across several routines. It is also important to keep each situation as natural as possible. This includes using materials natural to the task, and keeping normal distractions present. This will facilitate generalization. You may, of course, have to initially limit the distractions and structure the teaching environment somewhat, but these structural changes should be removed before you stop teaching a particular routine. It is important to make sure that students can perform routines under the conditions that are most natural in nontraining environments before moving on to other routines.

You will also want to shift the people your student interacts with on the various routines throughout the training sequence. It is important that students be able to communicate with a variety of other people. Adults and peers who communicate well should be available for your students to practice their new found skills. Careful changes in training personnel will assist you in achieving generalization.

3. Facilitating Initiated Communication

Another important consideration of programming is facilitating initiated communication. You must be willing to allow children to express their needs and wants, and to respond to each of their attempts at communication. This means that you will often have to assume a listener's role. Structure the environment to evoke approximations of the desired behavior and then wait until the child displays any level of communicative behavior that can be reinforced. Refrain from actively controlling when, where, and how much children can communicate, and allow them the opportunity to communicate freely throughout the day. Be aware of all the possible communication opportunities that might arise so that you can be ready to respond to them when they occur. You will need to train yourself to "think communication" in every activity throughout the day. This will take a mild transition from one who directs most of the activities to one who sets up structures to facilitate communication. When you have made this transition, you will increase the possibilities of your students becoming active participants in their social environments.

Facilitating initiated communication also requires that the classroom setting be structured in such a way that children must interact before receiving desired objects and activities. You must determine if your student's needs are currently being anticipated and met before an opportunity arises to communicate those needs. Teachers should recognize the danger in anticipating children's needs and the effect this has on their motivation to communicate. If children are given what they want without having to interact, there is little reason for them to communicate. This is a particularly significant concern for children who have no identifiable form and no identifiable intent (function). If children automatically get dessert at lunch time, they do not need to request it. Children will learn quickly that if enough time goes by, someone will see that dessert is served. Withholding those things you know your student wants or needs increases the motivation and opportunity to initiate interaction and communication.

4. Providing Consequences during Communication Sessions

All consequences used during programming should be as natural as possible. For each communication skill, identify the consequence that naturally follows the communication. If a child communicates that he or she is hungry, food is the natural consequence. If a child tells you he or she needs help, then help should be provided. These natural consequences should be used whenever possible during instruction. While the child is beginning to acquire a new communication skill, always try to respond to the communicative intent. Later, once the child has acquired the skill, you might not always want to (or be able to) respond to the communication. In cases where you cannot or do not want to respond to the request, you should acknowledge the communication and attempt to continue to converse with the child to maintain communicative contact. Often contact is broken off after a particular request has been refused, or after a student shows signs of displeasure upon being denied something that he or she wants. To help build communication skills in the students, you should continue the conversation whenever possible. If your student is behaving inappropriately, however, you will want to hold back your conversation until he or she is behaving more appropriately.

GUIDELINES FOR OVERALL COMMUNICATION PROGRAMS

The following guidelines are suggested for developing an overall communication program using a routine format:

1. Complete communication assessment on home and school inventories.
2. Identify and evaluate patterns of form and function use.
3. Prioritize communication goals for home and school for increasing functions.
4. Prioritize communication goals for home and school for increasing form sophistication and utility.
5. Determine long-term goals for inclusion on the individualized education program (IEP).
6. Determine short-term objectives and program targets.
7. Identify communication targets that can become whole routines.
8. Identify context situations during routines in which communication skills can be embedded.
9. Determine how you will provide the opportunity for communicating (structuring the situations).
10. Select the communication functions and forms you will teach. Remember to select a form that will not limit the child's audience, is acceptable to others, and at

the same time will produce immediate results for the child. Always keep the function intact when you focus on form.

EXAMPLE OF A COMMUNICATION ROUTINE

Communicating a Choice

Steps:

1. Go to choice board (felt board with pictures of items and activities available in area).
2. Point to choice.
3. Execute choice.
4. If time, return to choice board and repeat 1–3.

EXAMPLE OF A ROUTINE WITH COMMUNICATION SKILLS EMBEDDED

Changing into School Clothes before Snack

Steps:

1. Get school clothes.
2. Go to changing area.
   2a. *Sign "Help" to untie shoes.*[1]
3. Take gym shoes off.
4. Take gym socks off.
5. Take shorts off (for some children you will have to develop a smaller routine consisting of standing up, taking shorts down, sitting down, and then taking shorts off).
6. Take gym shirt off.
7. Put school shirt on.
8. Put pants on.
9. Put socks on.
10. Put on shoes.
    10a. *Sign "Help" to tie shoes.*
11. Put gym clothes on shelf.
12. Go to snack.

---

[1] Embedded communication forms are in italics for emphasis.

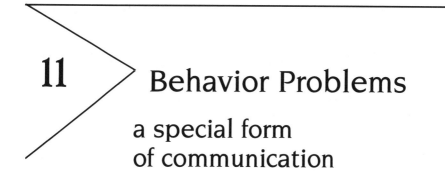

11 ⟩ Behavior Problems

a special form of communication

When you implement a student's routines, you may see undesirable behaviors. Often those behaviors are labeled behavior problems that need to be eliminated before the program can progress. They are frequently treated as something that is happening outside the current lesson. IMPACT takes a different view of these behaviors by treating them as diagnostic behaviors that tell us there is something wrong with the lesson in progress. In other words, they are a form of communication. Until we understand these attempts at communicating, we will not be able to make the necessary changes in our instruction to provide an effective instructional routine absent of problem behaviors. The child is letting you know that something is not being understood. Rather than beginning to set up control procedures to eliminate the problem behaviors, we need instead to ask the question, "What is the child trying to say to us?" By analyzing the communicative intent of a problem behavior episode during a routine, we can begin to develop alternate forms that the child can use. Correcting problem behaviors, then, becomes a communication program and the techniques outlined in Chapter 10, "Teaching Communication in Context," can be applied.

There is a temptation to treat problem behaviors as interruptions to the regular program, and many times they are. When these interruptions occur, it is common to search for underlying causes that exist outside the current routine. To be sure, the problem behavior may be caused by events outside the control of the teacher. Nevertheless, problem behaviors can best be dealt with in the context in which they occur. When a problem behavior occurs, a child is trying to produce an effect. The effect desired by the child may not be the one usually achieved by the routine in progress, and it may not even be the usual effect they try to achieve in this situation. It is, however, the most desired effect for that child at the moment. When a behavior is viewed as an attempt to communicate, you focus on understanding the communicative intent and shaping the form so that it is more acceptable to everyone.

Understanding the communicative intent of a child with moderate to severe handicaps is not an easy task. This is especially true when the child is trying to communicate with behaviors that are either dangerous or difficult to tolerate. Additionally, it is not always possible to accede to the request of the student. When considering problem behaviors as a communicative act, three general situations can occur:

1. The communicative intent (desired effect) is clear, and you can and will accede to the request.
2. The communicative intent is clear, but you cannot or will not accede to the request.
3. The communicative intent is unclear or indeterminable.

Each of these situations is discussed below. They are treated as separate situations for clarity, but in many situations all three may occur within a single routine or a set of related routines.

1. THE COMMUNICATIVE INTENT IS CLEAR, AND YOU CAN ACCEDE TO THE REQUEST

When the communicative intent is evident, and you are willing and able to respond to the request, the instructional problem becomes one of either shaping the existing form into one that is more acceptable, or substituting a new, more appropriate form that will achieve the same effect. It is important that each step used to go from the existing problem behavior to a more acceptable form allows the child to produce the desired effect. That will allow the new form to compete effectively with the undesired, problem behavior.

If you choose to shape the existing form, you must catch the behavior early. Often, there are precursor behaviors that precede the problem behavior that you can use as a first step. For example, some children will tap or bang a table before they erupt into a full blown tantrum with screaming, kicking, and wiggling away. If the tapping or banging can be used as the initial communicative form to shape, a majority of the tantrums will be virtually eliminated. (There will be some, of course, because you will not cue into the communication fast enough on every occasion.) Then you can shape the tapping or banging into a more reliable and universal form. It is very difficult to shape a new form after the tantrum has begun. In those cases, it is best to terminate the situation as soon as possible, and prepare to focus on a precursor the next time it occurs. Little productive instruction is accomplished during a tantrum, and a lot of energy and emotion are wasted trying to force a child to comply when he or she is obviously out of control.

Some people believe, "If you let a child get away with something, the child will never learn to behave." Where the function of tantrums is to escape, then it is true that tantrums will be reinforced when the child can escape a situation by tantruming. If, however, you view the tantrum as a communicative act, then what you have done is reinforced a communicative form that you would like to replace. If you develop another, more desirable, form that is *equally effective* in achieving the communicative effect for the child, it is likely to replace the tantrum. A good thing to remember is that each time you reinforce an undesired behavior (form), you have ensured yourself another instructional chance. Knowing that the same situation will reoccur, you will need to plan an alternate response that will strengthen the desired form and thereby eliminate the need for a tantrum.

There is another point to remember about shaping forms. The first form you select to reinforce may not be the final form you want the child to use to communicate.

Take the banging example above. Certainly, you would not like a child to bang the table every time he or she wants to say "no" or "I want to quit." You could, however, reinforce banging as an intermediate step toward a more conventional sign or pointing gesture. Banging is much easier to shape into a sign, and it is easier to tolerate than tantruming. Because it is easier to shape (and tolerate) you will increase the amount of time you can use to teach, and you will probably increase your effectiveness as well.

Sometimes it is easier to replace the problem behavior with another form. This is especially true when the problem behavior is particularly dangerous, or when you cannot find a reliable precursor, or when the precursor is not easily shaped into a useable communicative form. When you select your alternative form, be sure to select a form that you can be sure the child will exhibit. Physically prompted forms are usually preferred since you can prompt them rapidly and reliably. For example, a child in one of the IMPACT programs used to fall to the floor and bite the teacher when he did not want to do his work or eat his lunch. It was decided to prompt him to raise his hand when he wanted to quit or when he wanted us to leave. After close observation we saw that he would start to grind his teeth just before he bolted for the teacher's leg. Under the new program, once he began to grind his teeth, the teacher would quickly lift his hand, tell him it looked like he wanted to quit, and then she left him for a while. No biting occured. After a few trials, he began raising his hand on his own. The teacher acceded to his request, and the biting behavior disappeared. Later in the program, his hand raising could be shaped into different signs for various request like "go away," "stop," or "I want help."

You can look for acceptable alternatives from those behaviors that presently occur in other contexts. These may be your best alternatives since they are already in the repertoire of the child. Be sure to plan to develop multiple alternatives to each problem behavior. Good behavior is often ignored in the natural environment, so it is necessary to supply more than one way to achieve a communication goal and receive reinforcement. This emphasis on encouraging multiple responses will also aid children in generalizing and maintaining the skills that you teach.

2. THE COMMUNICATIVE INTENT IS CLEAR, BUT YOU CANNOT OR WILL NOT ACCEDE TO THE REQUEST

Where the communication is clear, but you cannot or will not accede to the wishes of the child, we have a slightly different instructional goal. The child must understand that he or she cannot do everything he or she wants and needs to learn acceptable ways to deal with disappointment or frustration. It is very important to acknowledge the communication even when you cannot accede to the demand. For example, when a child wants a ball and begins to cry, it is necessary to say "I know you want the ball, but it is time to go in now. When we finish dinner, you can come out and play again." This type of response acknowledges the communication so the child realizes that he or she has been understood, states a reason why the request cannot be acceded to, and specifies when and where the request can be met. When you choose to delay a response that meets a child's request, you must use short delays initially. Otherwise, the connection between the initial request and the communicative function will be lost. After the notion of delay is taught, you may begin lengthening the duration of the delays until a reasonable level is reached. Many children with moderate to severe handicaps will not respond to a statement of delay at first, but as their communicative intent is achieved through the form(s) in which you provide instruction, they will eventually learn that they were understood. After a number of times when they successfully achieve their desired intent following a short delay, they learn that they can communicate with you even though their requests will not always be immediately met. You will want to teach them ways to deal with this situation. For example, if the class is going outside, but a particular child wants to continue playing with a toy inside, you might show the child how he or she can take the toy outside. If this is not practical, you might be prepared to substitute another favored item that could be taken along.

It is very important to remember that no child will learn to deal effectively with rejection or denial without being successful a major proportion of the time. If the student you are teaching rarely gets his or her way, then it is unlikely that he or she will readily accept a denial from you. Most of us are willing to accept denials or frustration because we have enough successful experiences to teach us that the situation is unusual and that we will have success with other requests. Without a high percentage of success, the teaching process will be a long and tedious one. Often teachers and parents will slip into power interventions to make the child accept denial of a request. These power approaches may work in the short run with smaller and less persistent children, but they are rarely successful in the long run. Children will learn to accept denials and frustration ONLY after they have established confidence in their ability to influence what happens to them on a regular and consistent basis.

As the communication skills of your student improve, the student will naturally learn that he or she can influence what happens to him or her without resorting to tantrums or other disordered behaviors. Of course, the child still will get mad and behave inappropriately some of the time (we all do that on occasion), but the intensity and length of the tantrums will lessen as the child develops confidence in his or her communicative ability. Eventually, the student may even learn to handle disappointments without a major tantrum. When your routines are functional *for the child*, and communication is taught in context, the learning process will be accelerated.

3. THE COMMUNICATIVE INTENT IS UNCLEAR OR INDETERMINABLE

When the purpose of the child's problem behavior is unknown or unclear, you are presented with the hardest situation. When this occurs, you are virtually in the dark. You will need to resort to *hypothesis testing* to determine the intent of a particular behavior. This is especially difficult if your student uses the same general behavior for more than one intent.

The steps you take are straightforward. First, guess the purpose of the behavior (i.e., form a hypothesis). Such a guess can be developed on the basis of data collected on the occurrence of problem behavior at different times throughout the day (see Axelrod, 1987). Respond to the behavior as if it, in fact, indicated the intent you have chosen. Then collect data to determine if the tantrum or other behavior problem decreases or ceases. Use the data to determine if you have made the right choice. If you have, note the situation, the precursors of the behavior, and the specific action(s) you have taken. What you are doing is trying to guess the problem behavior's function, and to develop an alternative form to carry out that function. If you are correct, you will teach the child the new form that you used so that the problem behavior will no longer be a concern. If you are wrong, you will have to guess another function and try again.

Once you have discovered what alleviates the tantrum or other problem behavior, then that specific action or form becomes the beginning communication form you teach. You will want to develop a "word" for that action that can be *used by the child* to communicate the *same* intent in the future. The word you use can be a gesture, sign, picture, or whatever seems appropriate to the situation, and should be embedded into the action that you took. Remember, when you choose a particular communicative form for the child, you want to select a form that can be used universally.

Often in the heat of the situation you will try several different forms (critical elements) until you produce the desired response. For example, you may change the level of assistance, give several different verbal instructions, or change the task. Then you will have to establish which particular element was successful in communicating to the child. This is important, because the signal, cue, or sign you select to identify with your understanding of the child's communicative intent will become part of the child's own vocabulary. If you have not isolated the correct element of the successful communication, you will have the child merely producing linguistic noise that will inhibit successful communication in the future.

The following process will help you isolate the critical elements of the situation. Select the element(s) most likely to have made the difference, and use them exclusively the next time the problem behavior occurs. If they do not produce the same result, and you are relatively sure that the communicative intent is the same, then systematically introduce each additional element on subsequent occurrences of the problem behavior until you are successful. After a successful combination of elements has been found, eliminate as many as possible of the other elements that you tried, in order to determine the smallest combination of elements required to eliminate the problem behavior. Once the combination has been determined, use it as the desired form(s) to teach. Use the entire combination or sequence as a communicative form initially, and then shape it into a more efficient form after it has reliably replaced the problem behavior, always keeping the function intact. Accede to the communicative requests a majority of the time while this learning process is going on. Remember, until a child can communicate effectively, with a great deal of reliablity, and thereby influence life events, he or she will not readily accept denials or frustration. Of course, no one can always get what he or she wants anytime he or she wants it, but during acquisition of new skills, especially communication skills, it is important to ensure a high percentage of successful requests. You can introduce denial and postponing success later.

Traditional behavioral programs often produce what appears to be a similar effect. They reduce the undesirable behavior through various punishing techniques, and often attempt to build alternate noncommunicative responses in other training situations. These techniques do not, however, increase a child's ability to communicate, and the apparent success may be short-lived. Since the problem behavior was the major means of communication by the child, when the need to communicate similar intents arises, the problem behavior will probably reoccur, if you have not taught an alternate communicative form that is equally effective. Often you will not discover the error until you stop the training, change the structure of the classroom, or view the child in other settings with other people. This is another reason why it is essential to probe each routine in several natural environments throughout the instructional process.

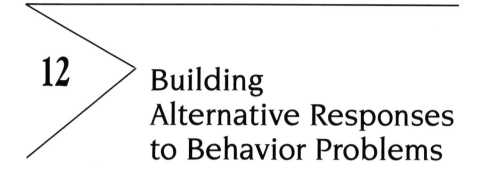

12 > Building Alternative Responses to Behavior Problems

A major focus of the IMPACT curriculum is the development of efficient communication. This involves the selection of a form that can be understood by others and that will reliably achieve the desired communicative function. Problem behaviors are often effective forms, regardless of whether or not the receiver is aware of their communicative intent. Take the situation where a child wants something to eat. If he or she signs or signals that a snack is wanted about 15 minutes before lunch or dinner, he or she is likely to be told to wait for dinner. (The same is true if a child signs for a drink or snack during a lesson at school.) If, on the other hand, the child begins to cry, bangs on the cupboards, or pulls on father's leg, he or she is more likely to get something to eat. This is especially true when the child persists or when the other party is busy with other activities. Each time these problem behaviors succeed, they are being reinforced as *communicative forms*. When these forms are reinforced often enough, and thereby appear frequently in the child's environments, they become labeled as a problem. Usually, once they are labeled as a problem, attempts are made to eliminate them. That is not a very productive approach. IMPACT philosophy indicates that since they are communicative behaviors, they need to be shaped or replaced instead of eliminated. This chapter shows you how to build alternative, desired responses from those that are labeled problem behaviors.

ANALYZING THE SITUATION

When you begin to analyze the learning situation, you will want to examine the state of affairs both before and after the child's problem behavior occurs. You should investigate what precedes the behavior, what others do in response to it, and what effect it produces for both the child and the person(s) who respond(s) to it in the situation. Four different types of situations can be identified when analyzing the situation in order to determine which alternative responses to develop. These four types of situations will give you a good starting place for planning your instruction. There is, of course, overlap between the categories, but they can be useful in directing your attention to critical program elements that might be altered first.

Type 1. When the Child Does Not Exhibit the Response You Want Used

When a child never responds the way you want him or her to, or when he or she is unable to apply a learned response to a particular situation, there is an antecedent problem. An antecedent problem exists when your attention needs to be directed to what happens prior to the behavior. Antecedent problems require that you give the child more information before the response occurs. In other words, if you have never seen your student display the desired form, then you will need to give him or her specific help to prompt the desired response. You may have to model or mold the desired response or provide a direct prompt that indicates what you want. In each case, the rule of thumb is that when you have not seen the response you want, you supply additional information.

Sometimes the child has shown you the behavior you want in other situations. For example, you might have a child who is able to ask for help when desiring to swing in the playground, but is unaware that that same skill could be used to get you to help him or her in opening a thermos. Again, you will want to provide antecedent information that will ensure the desired responses. This might be a prompt, a gesture, a verbal reminder, or some other form of stimulus change that will highlight the need for a particular response. What you are trying to do is to give the child enough help so that he or she can respond correctly. The help you give should be as natural as possible. The more artificial help you give, the more difficulty you will have in fading cues or prompts and the more problems you will have in getting the child to use the skills in other settings. (See Chapter 9, "The Instructional Process," for more details on the use of prompts and cues.)

Type 2. When the Child Does Not Use the Desired Form Consistently

Sometimes a routine is functional and you have given enough information for the child to respond correctly, but the child is not making sufficient progress. If the child can perform the task, but often does not, then you could have a reinforcement problem. Perhaps the child does not recognize that the effect or result of a successful routine will be rewarding. This may be the case for children who have not completed a routine very many times, or who have been taught a series of isolated small steps for artificial rewards. If the routines you use are carefully selected based on the inventories, and are functional for the child, this problem should be minimized. Once the child experiences success within a routine, his or her rate of responding should increase.

A common error in implementing routines is allowing the student to reach the intended reward without completing the steps required in the routine. Often, the child will begin a routine, engage in one or more problem behaviors that stop the flow of the routine, and then be allowed to reach the desired effect as a result of the problem behavior. It is important to limit the child's access to the desired rewards. Each student should only achieve the desired effect by completing the routine appropriately. If the child can only have access to the rewarding effect by performing the appropriate routine, his or her consistency should increase. Here is a point in instruction where problem behaviors can often pose serious difficulties for the teacher. If you are teaching a particular routine, and a problem behavior occurs that enables the child to achieve desired outcomes without completing the routine, the child will not learn the routine. Another situation that will have to be addressed is when a child does a routine at a pace that is so slow it is nonfunctional. Often we will tolerate a pace that would not be tolerated by others in the environment, or would not reach the desired goal in a reasonable amount of time. When this occurs, behavior problems are likely. If you provide the appropriate amount of assistance during the routine, these problems should be minimized. It is important to ensure a successful routine as often as possible. Well planned routines, efficiently implemented, will eliminate many potential problem areas.

Type 3. When Other Rewards Are Competing with the Routine

Routines will also not be very successful in situations where a child can have access to a different, but more powerful, reward outside of the routine. If your student reaches a particular step of a routine, stops the routine, and then engages in a problem behavior that ends the instruction and achieves another competing reward, progress on the routine will be slow. Often we respond to problem behaviors in ways that are more reinforcing than the routine's critical effect. When a child tries to gain access to another reward by ending or diverting the routine, you have a very critical choice to make. Remember, problem behaviors are considered attempts to communicate. A problem behavior could be indicating several different intents. It could mean, "I don't want to do this anymore," or "I can't do this part (particular step) without more help," or "I want something else now" (something else has become more appealing at this time). You need to be able to respond in most cases to the break in the routine by analyzing the communication, not eliminating the problem behavior or forcing completion of the routine. The hypothesis testing analysis used in Chapter 11, "Behavior Problems," will again aid you in determining what to do. Select the most likely intent, respond to it, and observe the result. If the child readily abandons the routine, you will need to make modifications in the instructional process. You may want to wait until he or she tires of the new activity, or increase the assistance at the problem step, or break the step down into smaller steps with the same amount of assistance, or even enhance the reward at the end of the routine. Enhancing the reward, however, should be done with caution. You do not want to add artificial elements that will have to be removed later on in the instructional process, unless absolutely necessary.

As pointed out in Chapter 9, "The Instructional Process," if the use of full physical assistance produces aggressive responses, a reduction in the level of assistance is appropriate. If the aggressive behavior is reduced consistently with the reduction in the level of assistance, then the routine should be continued as planned. If after several attempts, the child still continues to exhibit aggressive behaviors, then a change in the routine that reinterprets the critical effect, and communicative intent included, is required.

If you feel that the child simply does not want to perform the routine at all, you may want to schedule teaching it a little less often, or providing more time in between trials, or pairing it with another, more reinforcing, routine. Often the reward of a particular routine is not very strong for the child, but the routine is very important to the other caregivers in the environment. When a child exhibits a problem behavior, he or she is trying to tell you something. It may be that the child feels that what is required to go to the toilet is not worth the relief of not becoming soiled or the praise of another adult. It may be that to convert the problem routine into a successful one, you will have to follow it with another routine that is highly reinforcing like going outside or going for a snack.

Type 4.   Satiation: When a Routine Works too Well, too Often

As a child becomes more successful at reaching a particular critical effect, the value of that effect as a reinforcer may diminish. Imagine that you wanted a chocolate sundae. You might go to extensive lengths to get the first one. If, however, someone asked you to do some work for a second one, you would be less inclined. By the third or fourth one, your interest in working for ice cream would be greatly diminished. The same is true for children. If they need to finish a routine of dressing to get to go to the playground, they will be willing one or two times in a morning. If, however, you have several additional routines that lead to the same activity, the power of the reward will lessen. Behavior problems may arise in those situations where the interest in the critical effect that is achieved is lessened by satiation.

Another situation is where the child is tired of a particular activity. If this happens, you might want to change the activity for the sake of greater variety. Here you want to keep the same reward or critical effect, but develop another routine to reach it. Often we are so pleased to find one routine that works, we tend to overuse it. After you have found one routine that sucessfully leads to a desired result, develop a second and third one.

A Special Problem for Children with Autism

Most of us are required to do some things that are not pleasant or rewarding. We do them because we will gain some reward or avoid some discomfort. Often, the reward or discomfort comes from other people in our environment. Children with autism seldom form the types of social relationships that enable them to feel guilty for not performing or to feel satisfied by praise from others for doing a good job. Until these relationships are formed, you will have to ensure that the routines you use obtain access to desired rewards for the child. This may include the pairing of routines as outlined above, or even the reduction of expectations of some programs. You may even choose to add artificial reinforcers to the routine, but remember you will have to plan to fade them or shift them to the natural environment sometime in the future unless you want to include them as a permanent part of the routine. In other words, if you are unable to produce a desired routine in the natural environment without some artificial reward, consider the reward as part of the prosthetics that are required for that particular program. In this case, the natural reward for completing the routine is not important to the child, but is probably important to the adults in the environment. To prevent the overuse of artificial rewards, routines must be selected that are meaningful to the child and are feasible in the child's environment.

Selecting the correct response to problem behaviors is not easy. If you can remember that each problem behavior is a communicative one, you will develop a perspective on functional communication that will aid you in determining what needs to be done. Several different types of analyses were discussed in this chapter. Be aware of their implications when you are observing a routine and deciding what changes it needs.

This discussion of behavior problems will, of course, not equip you with everything you need to know. It is intended to be a set of guidelines to help you structure your analysis of behavior problems. Other books and articles on behavior management should be consulted to aid you in your efforts (Wolery, Bailey, & Sugai, 1988; Alberto & Troutman, 1986). It is very important that you translate behavior management principles into communication principles when working with children with moderate to severe handicaps. Far too often, behavior management programs focus on reducing or eliminating problem behaviors. This is not the direction your programs should take. You will have to use your most creative abilities and summon all the good teaching practices that you have learned if you intend to effectively teach children with moderate to severe handicaps. The concept of viewing behavior problems as undesired forms within a routine will give you the necessary framework for designing programs. A checklist is provided below to help you review your efforts and deal with problems that you might have overlooked.

PROBLEM BEHAVIOR ANALYSIS CHECKLIST

This checklist should be used as a guide for analyzing problem behaviors. If you work through this checklist for each routine, you should be able to spot what is wrong with the program. Then, refer to the text for ideas on how to change the routine.

1. Is the Task Functional for the Child in the Present Setting?

Often routines that are developed are not functional for the child. Many routines have only desired effects for the adult caregivers in the environment. If a problem behavior occurs during the initial implementation of a routine, check to see if the routine is really functional for the child.

2. Have You Carefully Specified the Level of Performance that You Want and the Procedures You Will Use?

Sometimes you will not be clear as to what is expected in a particular routine. Often in concentrating on getting a response out of a child, you will alter the instructions, add different steps, and accept different levels of performance. The result often is confusion for the student, which produces problem behaviors.

3. Are the Expected Levels of Performance Near the Child's Current Level of Functioning?

If you have selected an inappropriate degree of assistance for use during instruction, or have made a change in the routine that is beyond the ability of your student, you will often see problem behaviors. In this case, the level of performance expected should be adjusted until you determine the level where a majority of the problem behaviors will disappear.

4. Are Your Instructions Clear and Understood by the Child?

Be sure that you are clear when you give instructions and/or prompts and cues to a child. The beginning of the routine should be readily understood by the child. Often you will have to use a gesture or other prompt to signal a particular step.

5. Do the Cues and Prompts Exist in the Natural Environment?

Here the problem rests in the transference from training to nontraining settings. The cues used in training to signal the beginning of a routine or to identify a particular step need to be similar to ones that occur in the student's other environments.

6. Are You Varying the Amount and Types of Rewards that You Are Using?

Often problem behaviors occur when there is a change in the level or type of reward. A student is used to receiving a certain reward, and, when it changes, he or she exhibits problem behaviors to try to return to the previous situation. Be sure that the levels of reward are faded in small steps, and that the routine can be performed fluently before you begin fading the amount of reward. This type of problem also can occur when delays are introduced into intructional plans. Again, care should be taken to ensure the timely completion of a routine to minimize problem behaviors.

7. Has There Been a Shift in the Amount of Reinforcement Due to Program Changes or Increased Performance?

Often children with moderate to severe handicaps have problems changing situations or assignments. They may exhibit problem behaviors when you ask them to return to work or go somewhere they do not want to go. This can be viewed as a change in reward. The child was able to get the immediate reward desired in a free situation, and now you are putting restrictions on his or her behavior. If this occurs, you will want to set up quick, short routines that will enable the child to return to a desired reward. As the student becomes familiar with these new routines, you may lengthen them. This will enable you to increase his or her performance without problem behaviors by increasing their ability to earn the desired reward.

8. Is the Child Satiated with the Reward?

When you use the same routine frequently, or when a previously unsuccessful routine becomes successful, the student can become satiated on the reward. When this happens, either space out the number of times you use that routine, or enter other routines that will lead to different rewards between trials.

9. Are You Still Using an Enthusiastic Delivery of Instructions and Rewards?

Sometimes after you have been teaching a particular activity or routine a number of times your enthusiasm declines. An effective remedy is to transfer the routine to someone else, design a different routine to reach the same critical effect, or stop the routine for a few days to refresh both your and your student.

10. Are the Rewards a Natural Consequence of the Routine?

Be sure that the routines you design actually do achieve a critical effect for the child. Not doing this is one of the major mistakes in developing routines. We all tend to develop routines that we think children should learn for our own purposes rather than routines that will gain access to rewards for the child.

11. Have You Programmed More than One Alternative Acceptable Behavior?

When designing a routine, attempt to include more that one set of behaviors to reach a critical effect. If you program only one way to reach a goal, you will often hinder generalization. Additionally, if the only way taught is not working, your student may resort to problem behaviors to escape the situation.

12. Have You Carefully Analyzed the Context of the Behavior Problem?

If the above modifications do not work to reduce the problem behaviors, then you will need to analyze the context of the problem carefully. A video tape of the situation is often a good source for determining that context. If you do not have a tape, you can ask someone to watch you or you can watch while someone else runs your program.

13. Have You Looked for Alternative Forms that the Child Uses in Other Contexts?

Many times it is difficult to determine which routine, or which steps within a routine, to use. A valuable source of forms to use are other situations where you can observe the child. Looking for alternative forms that are already in the child's repertoire will often speed up the process of designing or modifying routines.

14. Have You Collected Specific Data on Your Trials and Errors To Be Able To Decide What the Child is Trying To Communicate?

A final technique that can help you with problem behaviors is the careful collection of data around a problem situation. The use of empirical data to determine communicative intent cannot be overemphasized. If you develop your observation skills and increase your ability to speculate about what the child might be saying in this situation, you will enhance your design capabilities. It is very difficult to extract meaning from behavior. Experience is a major ingredient in this process. A successful routine designer will develop the skill of mixing intuition and data analysis into the process of program design.

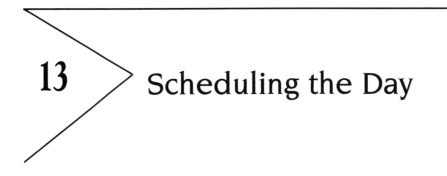

13 ▷ Scheduling the Day

The following are two examples to assist you in developing schedules for your classroom. There is no one way to schedule with the IMPACT curriculum. Each classroom schedule will vary depending on the children in the classroom and their particular priorities, the staff available for programming, and other resources (e.g., money, transportation) that can be provided by your district or developed by you.

The two sample schedules were drawn from the schedules of IMPACT demonstration classrooms. The first schedule was for a classroom of younger children who required a great deal of assistance in completing everyday routines. The second was for a classroom of older children who were learning more complicated routines required in adult living. Before each schedule, there is a brief description of the children in the classroom and some information about how programming was done.

CLASSROOM SCHEDULE FOR YOUNGER CHILDREN

The classroom for younger children (see Figure 13.1) consisted of a teacher, a full-time aide, and six young children. The children lacked independence in all necessary routines—they were not toilet-trained, were unable to move from one activity to another without physical guidance, could not dress and undress themselves or perform other self-help skills, and had very limited communication skills that tended to be inappropriate or unconventional.

Basic routines and communication skills were priorities for the children. Each child initially required assistance in completing routines, so programming was staggered. A lot of time was spent on instruction in group activities and independent play. Once the children became more independent with basic routines, less time was required for these programs. New programming targets were then added.

Note that this teacher made use of normal peer tutors for some periods each day. During recess, a peer tutor worked with each child on targeted recreation goals. The teacher allotted 5 minutes to probe each child to determine his or her growth. At lunch, nonhandicapped peers joined in the family style lunch, and during gym a peer tutor assisted each child in using the gym equipment. Every Friday for half a day parents and volunteers took the students into the community to work on routines.

STUDENT	1	2	3	4	5	6
9:00–9:30	Request help with coat zipper; sign "toy"; greeting[1]	Request help with coat; sign "toy"; greeting[1]	OFF BUS: to classroom: put away materials; to play area Greeting; point to desired toy[1]	Greeting; point to desired toy[1]	Greeting; point to desired toy[1]	Greeting; sign "toy"[1]
9:30–9:40	Toilet: sign "toilet," request help (snap)[1]	Toilet: sign toilet, request help (with towel)[1]				
9:40–9:50	Play Area: independent & cooperative play		Toilet: Point to picture of toilet, request help getting towel[1]	Toilet: Sign "toilet," request help (belt buckle)[1]	PLAY AREA: independent and cooperative play	
9:50–10:00			PLAY AREA: independent and cooperative play		Toilet: Sign "toilet," request help (pants)[1]	Toilet: sign "toilet," request help (getting towel)[1]
10:00–10:25	10:00–10:15: go to kitchen for snack tray,		PREPARATION FOR SNACK 10:00–10:15: play area		10:00–10:15: set up chairs	10:00–10:15: play area
	10:15–10:25: wait at table		10:15–10:25: pass out napkins	10:15–10:25: pass out plates	10:15–10:25: wait at table	10:15–10:25: pass out utensils
10:25–10:40	SNACK: Teacher holds food and drink before children; must request to receive food or drink (structured communication period) Point to desired snack items	Request desired snack items	Locate picture of food/drink item in communication book	Request desired snack items	Point to desired snack items	Request desired snack items

Time					
10:40–10:50	Clear table			Wait at table	Toilet
10:50–11:00	Toilet			Wait at table	Toilet
11:00–11:20	Wash dishes	Rinse/stack dishes	Toilet; brush teeth	Toilet; wash face	Music in play area
11:20–11:30	Request help (coat)[1]		Request help (coat)[1]	PREPARE FOR RECESS: Coats on; line up at door	
11:30–12:00	Bike riding 11:30–11:45	Roller skating 11:35–11:40	Use teeter-totter 11:40–11:45	Use swing 11:45–11:50	Use slide 11:50–11:55
			RECESS WITH NORMAL PEERS		
12:00–12:15	LUNCH PREPARATION: hang up coats; wash hands; line up at door; walk to cafeteria				
12:15–12:25	Get food trays from kitchen	Pass out napkins	Pass out plates	Pass out cups	Pass out utensils
12:25–12:45	EAT LUNCH: pass food around; serve self family style (with nonhandicapped peers)				
12:45–1:00	AFTER LUNCH CLEAN-UP: each child scrapes and stacks dirty dishes on trays; throws out garbage				
	Tray to kitchen	Wipe table	Sweep floor	Wait at table	
1:00–1:05	Mobility to class				
1:05–1:20	Toilet; brush teeth	Toilet; comb hair	PLAY AREA: Independent play	Dress for gym, request help with dressing[1]	Request help with dressing[1]
1:20–1:35	PLAY AREA: independent play		Request help with dressing[1]	Toilet; wash face	Toilet; brush teeth

Figure 13.1. Classroom schedule for younger children.

(continued)

Figure 13.1. (continued)

STUDENT	1	2	3	4	5	6
1:35–1:50	Dress for gym, request help with dressing[1] (To gym)	Request help with dressing[1] (To gym)	Toilet; brush teeth (To gym)	Toilet; wash face (To gym)	(To gym)	PLAY AREA: independent play
1:50–2:05	GYM: with normal peers					
2:05–2:10	Mobility to class					
2:10–2:25			Group activity: art, music, film		Change gym clothes, request help with dressing[1]	Request help with dressing[1]
2:25–2:40	Group activity		Change gym clothes	Request help with dressing[1]		Group activity
2:40–2:55	Change gym clothes request help with dressing[1]	request help with dressing[1]			Group activity	
2:55–3:05	PLAY AREA: independent and cooperative play		PLAY AREA: independent and cooperative play		Toilet	
3:05–3:15	Toilet	Toilet		PLAY AREA: independent and cooperative play		Toilet
3:15–3:25	PLAY AREA: independent and cooperative play		Toilet	Toilet	PLAY AREA: independent and cooperative play	
3:25–3:30	PREPARE FOR HOME: coats on, line up at door					

Note: Fridays are community access days with parents and volunteers.
[1]Communication/social targets.

122

STUDENT	1	2	3	4	5	6
9:00–9:15	OFF BUS: to classroom; put away materials; to play area					
9:15–9:25	M: Get breakfast from kitchen W, TH: Independent tasks T: Set table F: Attendance slips to office	W, F: Independent tasks M: Set table T: Attendance to office TH: Get breakfast from kitchen	M: Attendance to office T, F: Independent tasks W: Set table F: Get breakfast from kitchen	M, T: Independent tasks W: Attendance to office F: Set table T: Get breakfast from kitchen	M, T: Independent tasks TH: Set table W: Gather laundry F: Pick up attendance slips from office	M, T: Independent tasks TH: Attendance to office W: Get breakfast from kitchen
9:25–9:30	Wash hands; to table					
9:30–9:50	Eat breakfast, family style Request/passing food; appropriate table manners; conversation[1] (teacher directed[2])					
9:50–10:05 (clear table/stack dishes; wipe tables, chairs; sweep) Other routines: hygiene	M: Clear table/stack T: Dry/put away dishes W: Rinse/stack dishes Th: Wash dishes F: Sweep floor	M: Wipe tables/chairs T: Clear table/stack W: Dry/put away dishes Th: Rinse/stack dishes F: Wash dishes	M: Sweep floor T: Wipe tables W: Clear table/stack Th: Dry/put away dishes F: Rinse/stack dishes	M: Wash dishes T: Sweep floors W: Wipe tables and chairs Th: Clear table/stack dishes F: Dry/put away dishes	M: Rinse/stack dishes T: Sweep floors W: Wipe table/chairs F: Clear table/stack dishes	M: Dry/put away dishes T: Rinse/stack W: Wash dishes Th: Sweep floor F: Wipe table/chairs
10:05–10:20 (Wash/rinse/dry/put away dishes) Other routines: hygiene	HYGIENE: Brush/floss teeth, wash face, use deodorant, comb hair, shave (In the 9:50–10:05 period, three children will clear table/stack dishes, wipe tables/chairs, sweep, while the others do hygiene routines. In the 10:05–10:20 period, the three children working on breakfast clean-up begin their hygiene routine, while the others complete the breakfast clean-up.)					
10:20–10:40	Mainstream: Shop	M,T,W,F: community money skills—rehearsal strategies TH: menu planning for next week's breakfast			Janitorial crew[2]: lunchroom clean-up	
10:40–11:00	Mainstream: Shop	Janitorial crew[2]: playground clean-up		M,T,W,F: community money skills—rehearsal strategies TH: menu planning for next week's lunch		
11:00–11:20	Group table games					

Figure 13.2. Classroom schedule for older children.

(continued)

123

Figure 13.2. *(continued)*

STUDENT	1	2	3	4	5	6
11:20–11:30			Dress for gym, to gym			
11:30–11:50			GYM: Basketball, relay races, and so forth[1] (with peer tutors)			
12:00–12:20			MONDAY–THURSDAY: Lunch preparation Wash hands, each prepare own sandwich, select fruit, drink, and so forth; put away food FRIDAYS: everyone assists in preparing hot meal			
12:20–12:50			Eat Lunch Appropriate table manners; conversation (teacher directed)			
12:50–1:00 (clear table/ stack dishes; wipe tables, chairs; sweep) OTHERS: Hygiene	F: wipe tables/ chairs	F: Sweep floor	LUNCH CLEAN-UP MONDAY–THURSDAY: everyone clears and washes own dishes F: Wash dishes	F: rinse/stack dishes	F: dry/put away dishes	F: clear table/stack dishes
1:00–1:10 (Wash/rinse/ dry/put away dishes) OTHERS: Hygiene			HYGIENE: brush teeth, wash face, comb hair			
1:10–1:30			Mobility to community site			
1:30–3:00	TH: Vocational placement site W: Laundromat, in- dependent tasks	TH: community site (i.e., museum, park, zoo)	MONDAY: Public library TUESDAY: shopping for groceries, personal items W: Laundry mat, independent FRIDAY: shopping for groceries, personal items	TH: Vocational placement site	TH: Community site (i.e., museum, park, zoo)	
3:00–3:15			Mobility back to school			
3:15–3:30			CLEAN ROOM: prepare to go home			

[1]Communication/social targets.
[2]Person(s) responsible for time period.

CLASSROOM SCHEDULE FOR OLDER CHILDREN

The classroom for older children (see Figure 13.2) consisted of a teacher, a full-time aide, and six adolescents. The children could perform most of their self-help routines (except for some hygiene tasks) independently, and a few children were quite verbal, although they tended to have a high rate of inappropriate verbalizations.

Priorities for these students consisted of community residence skills (independent or group home), community access skills (e.g., shopping, banking, use of community facilities), recreation/leisure skills, and appropriate interaction skills. Nonhandicapped peers assisted during gym with group games such as basketball, baseball, and other available recreation activities like golf, tennis, and handball. Two of the adolescents were targeted for a vocational placement. They attended a practicum placement once a week with the aide. Throughout the day, different students were responsible for telling when a programming segment was over. This helped provide training in management skills in a context similar to that in which the skills would be used in the community.

References

Alberto, P.A., & Troutman, D.C. (1986). Applied behavior analysis for teachers (2nd ed.). Columbus, OH: Charles E. Merrill.

Axelrod, S. (1987). Functional and structural analyses of behavior: Approaches to teaching reduced use of punishment procedures. *Research in Developmental Disabilities*, 8, 165–178.

Bambara, L.M., Warren, S.F., & Komisar, S. (1988). The individualized curriculum sequencing model: Effects on skill acquisition and generalization. *Journal of The Association for Persons with Severe Handicaps*, 13, 8–19.

Barrett, B.H. (1979). Communitization and the measured message of normal behavior. In R.L. York & E. Edgar (Eds.), *Teaching the severely handicapped* (Vol. IV) (pp. 301–318). Seattle, WA: American Association for the Education of the Severely/Profoundly Handicapped.

Baumgart, D., Brown, L., Pumpian, I., Nisbet, J., Ford, A., Sweet, M., Messina, R., & Schroeder, J. (1982). Principle of partial participation and individualized adaptations in educational programs for severely handicapped students. *Journal of The Association for the Severely Handicapped*, 7(2), 17–27.

Bellamy, G.T. (1976). Habilitation of the severely and profoundly retarded: A review of research on work productivity. In G.T. Bellamy (Ed.), *Habilitation of severely and profoundly retarded adults*, (Vol. 1). Eugene, Oregon: University of Oregon Center on Human Development.

Bendersky, M., Edgar, E., & White, O.R. (1977). Uniform performance assessment system. In N.G. Haring (Ed.), *The experimental education training program: An inservice program for personnel serving the severely handicapped: Vol. 1. Systematic Instruction* (pp. 37–52). Seattle, WA: University of Washington Press.

Billingsley, F.F. (1984). Where are the generalized outcomes? (An examination of instructional objectives). *Journal of The Association for Persons with Severe Handicaps*, 9, 186–192.

Billingsley, F.F. (1988). Writing objectives for generalization. In N. G. Haring (Ed.), *Generalization for students with severe handicaps: Strategies and solutions* (pp. 123–128). Seattle, WA: University of Washington Press.

Billingsley, F.F., & Liberty, K. A. (1982). The use of time-based data in instructional programs for the severely handicapped. *Journal of The Association for the Severely Handicapped*, 7(1), 47–55.

Billingsley, F.F., & Neel, R.S. (1985). Competing behaviors and their effects on skill generalization and maintenance. *Analysis and Intervention in Developmental Disabilities*, 5(4), 357–372.

Billingsley, F.F., & Romer, L.T. (1983). Response prompting and transfer of stimulus control: Methods, research, and a conceptual framework. *Journal of The Association for the Severely Handicapped*. 8(2), 3–12.

Brown, L., Branston, M.B., Hamre-Nietupski, S., Pumpian, I., Certo, N., and Gruenwald, L. (1979). A strategy for developing chronological age appropriate and functional curricular content for severely handicapped adolescents and young adults. *Journal of Special Education*, 13(1), 81–90.

Donnellan, A.M., & Neel, R.S. (1986). New directions in educating students with autism. In R.H. Horner, L.H. Meyer, & H.D.B. Fredericks (Eds.), *Education of learners with severe handicaps: Exemplary service strategies* (pp. 99–126). Baltimore: Paul H. Brookes Publishing Co.

Falvey, M., Brown, L., Lyon, S., Baumgart, D., & Schroeder, J. (1980). In W. Sailor, B. Wilcox, & L. Brown (Eds.), *Methods of instruction for severely handicapped students* (pp. 109–134). Baltimore: Paul H. Brookes Publishing Co.

Ferster, C.B. (1961). The development of performance in autistic children in an automatically controlled environment. *Journal of Chronic Diseases*, 13, 312–345.

Freagon, S., Pajor, M., Brankin, G., Galloway, A., Rich, D., Karel, P.J., Wilson, M., Costello, D., Peters, W.M., & Hurd, D. (1981). *Teaching severely handicapped students in the community.* Dekalb, Illinois: Northern Illinois University & DeKalb County Special Education Association.

Gesell, A., & Amatruda, C.S. (1949). *Gesell developmental schedules.* New York: Psychological Corporation.

Gold, M. (1973). Research on the vocational habilitation of the retarded: The present, the future. In N. Ellis (Ed.), *International review of research in mental retardation* (Vol.6, pp. 97–148). New York: Academic Press, Inc.

Haring, N.G. (Ed.). (1988). *Generalization for students with severe handicaps: Strategies and solutions.* Seattle, WA: University of Washington Press.

Horner, R.H. (1988, May). Functional analysis in applied settings. In A.J. Cuvo (Chair), *Behavior analysis of community referenced skills: Issues in promoting and transferring stimulus control.* Symposium conducted at the fourteenth annual convention of the Association for Behavior Analysis. Philadelphia.

Horner, R.H., & Bellamy, G.T. (1979). Structured Employment: Productivity and Productive Capacity. In G.T. Bellamy, G. O'Conner, and O.C. Karan (Eds.), *Vocational rehabilitation of severely handicapped persons* (pp. 85–101). Baltimore, MD: University Park Press.

Horner, R.H., & Billingsley, F.F. (1988). The effect of competing behavior on the generalization and maintenance of adaptive behavior in applied settings. In R.H. Horner, G. Dunlap, & R. Koegel (Eds.), *Generalization and maintenance: Life-style changes in applied settings* (pp. 197–220). Baltimore: Paul H. Brookes Publishing Co.

Horner, R.H., McDonnell, J.J., & Bellamy, G.T. (1986). Teaching generalized skills: General case instruction in simulation and community settings. In R.H. Horner, L.H. Meyer, & H.D.B. Fredericks (Eds.), *Education of learners with severe handicaps: Exemplary service strategies* (pp. 289–314). Baltimore: Paul H. Brookes Publishing Co.

Kayser, J.E., Billingsley, F.F., & Neel, R.S. (1986). A comparison of in-context and traditional instructional approaches: Total task, single trial versus backward chaining, multiple trials. *Journal of The Association for Persons with Severe Handicaps, 11,* 28–38.

Knapczyk, D.R. (1975). Task analytic assessment of severe learning problems. *Education and Training of the Mentally Retarded, 10,* 74–77.

Koegel, R.L., Rincover, A., & Egel, A.L. (1982). *Educating and understanding autistic children.* San Diego: College-Hill Press.

Lovaas, O.I. (1968). Some studies on the treatment of childhood schizophrenia. In J.M. Schlein (Eds.), *Research in psychotherapy* (Vol. 3). Washington, D.C.: American Psychological Association.

Lovaas, O.I., Koegel, R.L., Simmons, J.Q., & Long, J.S. (1973). Some generalization and followup measures on autistic children in behavior therapy. *Journal of Applied Behavior Analysis, 6,* 131–166.

Lovaas, O.I., Scheaffer, B., & Simmons, J. Q. (1965). Experimental studies in childhood schizophrenia: Building social behavior in autistic children by the use of electric shock. *Journal of Experimental Research in Personality, 1,* 99–109.

Lucas, E.V. (1980). *Semantic and pragmatic language disorders assessment and remediation.* Rockville, MD: Aspen Systems Corporation.

Neel, R.S., Billingsley, F.F., & Lambert, C. (1983). IMPACT: A functional curriculum for educating autistic youth in natural environments. In R. B. Rutherford, Jr. (Ed.), *Monograph in behavioral disorders: Severe behavior disorders of children and youth* (Series No. 6, pp. 40–50). Reston, VA: Council for Children with Behavioral Disorders.

Nietupski, J., Schuetz, G., & Ockwood, L. (1980). The delivery of communication therapy services to severely handicapped people: A plan for a change. *Journal of The Association for the Severely Handicapped, 5,* 13–23.

Pelland, M., & Falvey, M.A. (1986). Instructional strategies. In M. A. Falvey, *Community-Based curriculum: Instructional strategies for students with severe handicaps* (pp. 31–60). Baltimore: Paul H. Brookes Publishing Co.

Piaget, J. *The psychology of intelligence* (M. Piercy & D.E. Berlyne Trans.). London: Routledge & Kegan Paul Ltd. (Original work published 1947.)

Sailor, W., Guess, D., Goetz, L., Schuler, A., Utley, B., and Baldwin, M. (1980). Language and severely handicapped persons. In W. Sailor, B. Wilcox, & L. Brown (Eds.), *Methods of instruction for severely handicapped students.* Baltimore: Paul H. Brookes Publishing Co.

Schopler, E. (1976). Towards reducing behavior problems in autistic children. In L. Wing (Ed.), *Early childhood autism: Clinical, education, and social aspects, 6,* 23–29.

Stokes, T.F., & Baer, D.M. (1977). An implicit technology of generalization. *Journal of Applied Behavior Analysis, 10,* 349–367.

van den Pol, R.A., Iwata, B.A., Ivancic, M.T., Page, T.J., Neef, N.A., & Whitley, F.P. (1981). Teaching the handicapped to eat in public places: Acquisition, generalization, and maintenance of restaurant skills. *Journal of Applied Behavior Analysis, 20*(4), 61–69.

White, O.R. (1980). Adaptive performances objectives. In W. Sailor, B. Wilcox, & L. Brown (Eds.), *Methods of instruction for severely handicapped students* (pp. 47–69). Baltimore: Paul H. Brookes Publishing Co.

White, O. R. (1985). Decisions, decisions. . . . B.C. *Journal of Special Education, 9,* 305–320.

White, O.R. (1988). Probing skill use. In N.G. Haring, (Ed.), *Generalization for students with severe handicaps: Strategies and solutions.* Seattle, WA: University of Washington Press, 131–141.

Wing, L. (1981). Language, social, and cognitive impairments in autism and severe mental retardation. *Journal of Autism and Developmental Disorders,* 11(1), 31–44.

Wolery, M., Bailey, D.B. Jr., & Sugai, G.M., (1988). *Effective teaching: Principles and procedures of applied behavior analysis with exceptional students.* Boston: Allyn & Bacon.

Wolery, M., & Gast, D.L. (1984). Effective and efficient procedures for the transfer of stimulus control. *Topics in Early Childhood Special Education,* 4(3), 52–57.

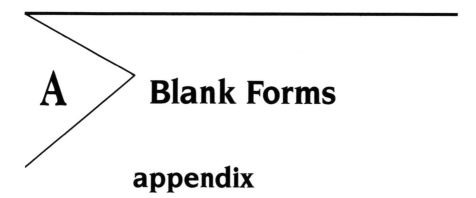

A Blank Forms

appendix

IMPACT PARENT INTERVIEW FORM

Curricular components	Parents' concerns and comments
Inventories	
Instructional environments	
Parent involvement	
Function/form	
Communication functions	
Routines	
How classroom will change	
Role of other professionals	
Risks	
Generalization probes	

IMPACT PRIORITY SUMMARY SHEET

Overall Short-Term Priority List

Parent(s)	Agr.[1]	Teacher(s)

Critical Priority List

Parent(s)	Agr.	Teacher(s)

IEP Tentative Goal List

[1]Agr. = agreement. Check this column when parents and teachers agree on priority.

IMPACT COMMUNICATION
FORM SELECTION SUMMARY SHEET

Name: _____   Date: _____

Enter the form(s) selected for each of the functions listed below. The forms listed here should be the desired forms that you intend to include in your IEP goals and objectives. You may choose to use the same form with different activities within the same general function. For example, you may want to develop a two-word sentence for the ask function. The one form used to ask would be the same in all three ask functions listed on the sheet.

Function	Form (describe)
Ask, food	
Ask, activity	
Ask, outside	
Indicate injury	
Help, get things	
Help, find things	
Help, do something	
Ask directions	
Protest, activity	
Protest, food	
Protest, object	
Respond, family	
Respond, adults	
Respond, peers	
Initiate interaction, family	
Initiate interaction, adults	
Initiate interaction, peers	
Continue interaction, family	
Continue interaction, adults	
Continue interaction, peers	
Seek affection	
Seek reward	
Express interest	
Relate past events	
Pretend, Fantasy	

Assessment Data Sheet

Manager: _____

Name: _____
Date: _____
Routine: _____
Beginning natural cue: _____
Critical effect: _____
Latency: _____ Duration of routine: _____

Types of assistance:
FP = Full physical assistance
PA = Partial physical assistance
G = Gestural cue
V = Directive verbal cue
I = Natural cue or independent
ED = Duration error; Ⓒ = Communication target

Steps	Duration	Date	Date	Date	Type of assistance for instruction (describe)

Instructional Data Sheet

Manager: _____

Name: _____

Routine: _____

Date: _____

Beginning natural cue: _____

Critical effect: _____

Latency: _____ Duration of routine: _____

Dura-tion	Step	Assistance	Date	Date	Date	Assistance	Date	Date	Date

Total duration:

Ⓒ = Communication target

EL = Latency error
E = Response form error
ED = Duration error
C = Correct

Program changes:
/ = Change in assistance
// = Change in consequence

137

Instructional Conditions and Comments

Objective

_____

_____

Manager (parent, teacher, other supervisory individual)

_____

Conditions (appropriate times and situations)

_____

_____

_____

Comments, special instructions

_____

_____

_____

_____

138

Instructional Data Sheet (Short Form)

Page # _____

Name: _____

Routine: _____

Latency: _____

Assistance	Date	Date	Date	Assistance	Date	Date	Date

Total duration:

SAMPLE COVER LETTER TO PARENTS

Your name
Your address

Date

Dear Parent(s),

We are beginning to use a more functional curriculum at (your school) for children like your (son or daughter). The features of this new curriculum are outlined in *A Parent Guide to Understanding the IMPACT Curriculum* included with this letter.

One of the major improvements provided by this curriculum is the inclusion of the *IMPACT Environmental Inventory for Home and Community*. This inventory will provide essential information for us to be able to plan the most effective program for your (son or daughter). The role of providing detailed assessment information may be new to you, and the inventory may seem long, but the information you provide is the *most* important information we can get about what your child needs.

Please take time to read the Parent Guide and complete the enclosed inventory for your (son or daughter). We are enthusiastic about this new curriculum, and we are especially excited about the upcoming joint planning we will be doing for (child's name). If you have any questions or need help, please feel free to call me at (your telephone number).

Sincerely,

Your name
Telephone number repeated

B ▷ IMPACT
Environmental Inventory for Home and Community

appendix

PART 1

INVENTORY for _____

Sex _____ Age _____ School _____

Personal Information

Mother's name: _____ Age: _____

Father's name: _____ Age: _____

Address (if different from mother's): _____

City _____ State _____ Zip _____

Telephone: Mother (H): (   )   -   (W): (   )   -

Father (H): (   )   -   (W): (   )   -

Brothers and sisters (*list oldest first*):

Name: _____ Age: _____

Sex: _____ Live at home? _____

Relationship (biological, half, step): _____

Name: _____ Age: _____

Sex: _____ Live at home? _____

Relationship (biological, half, step): _____

Name: _____ Age: _____

Sex: _____ Live at home? _____

Relationship (biological, half, step): _____

Name: _____ Age: _____

Sex: _____ Live at home? _____

Relationship (biological, half, step): _____

Name: _____ Age: _____

Sex: _____ Live at home? _____

Relationship (biological, half, step): _____

Where Does Your Child Go?

One of the main parts of your child's program is to increase the number of places where he or she can go. This part of the questionnaire tells us about the places you and your child visit and how well he or she does in different places with different people and gives you an opportunity to tell us what specific problems your child has in various situations.

How often does your child play outside?

_____ Frequently   _____ Occasionally   _____ Never

Where does your child usually play when outside? If your child plays in more than one place on a *regular* basis, please tell us about how much time is spent in each place.

In your own yard? _____ Hrs. _____

Is your yard fenced? _____ Yes   _____ No

In neighborhood outside yard? _____ Hrs. _____

In a park or school ground? _____ Hrs. _____

When your child does play outside, how much supervision does he or she require?

_____ My child can play independently

_____ My child will play outside with family members

_____ My child will play outside with friends or neighbors

What types of problems, if any, does your child present when playing outside (e.g., runs away, tears at plants and eats them, hits other children, runs out into traffic)?

_____

_____

_____

Which community/recreation settings (e.g., playground, pool) does your child use?

_____

_____

_____

When your child goes to a community recreation setting, what amount of direct supervision is required? *(Check all that apply.)*

_____ None (independent)

_____ With family members

_____ With friends or neighbors

What community services (e.g., restaurants, stores, house of worship) does your child use?

_____

_____

_____

_____

When your child does use community services, what level of direct supervision is required? *(Check all the apply.)*

_____ None (independent)

_____ With family members

_____ With friends or neighbors

Are there places that you or other members of the family go where you usually would not take your child?

_____ Yes   _____ No

If yes, where? _____

_____

_____

What problems are created when he or she does go along?

_____

_____

_____

What skills does your child need to learn before you would feel comfortable letting him or her go *with you* on a regular basis? If the problems are different in different situations, please list each separately. *(Attach a separate sheet if you need more space.)*

_____

_____

_____

_____

What skills would your child have to learn to be able to go to these places *alone*? If the skills needed are different in different situations, please list each separately. *(Attach a separate sheet if you need more space.)*

_____

_____

_____

_____

_____

Does your child like to ride in a car? _____ Yes   _____ No

What problems occur, if any, when you go on a:

Short ride (5–15 minutes) _____

_____

Long ride (15 minutes or more) _____

_____

_____

What Does Your Child Do Most of the Time?

This section is designed to give us an idea about the number and types of activities your child participates in during the week. We are interested in where, when, and with whom your child interacts. We especially want to know the problems you and your child face on a day-to-day basis. Be sure to add any additional comments you feel will help us understand what goes on during a typical week. This information will be used to aid us in designing a functional program for your child.

What does your child usually do between school and dinner?

_____

_____

_____

Which of these activities does your child do:

Independently _____

With members of the family _____

_____

With friends and/or neighbors _____

_____

What special problems, if any, occur during those times?

_____

_____

_____

What does your child usually do between dinner and bedtime?

_____

_____

_____

Which of those activities does your child do:

Independently _____

With members of the family _____

_____

With friends and/or neighbors _____

_____

What special problems, if any, occur during those times?

_____

_____

_____

What does your child usually do on weekends?

_____

_____

_____

Which of those activities does your child do:

Independently _____

With members of the family _____

_____

With friends and/or neighbors _____

_____

What special problems, if any, occur during those times?

_____

_____

_____

Does your child play with other children? ____ Yes ____ No

If yes, with whom?

_____

_____

_____

What activities does your family do for entertainment *at home?*

_____

_____

_____

_____

Which activities does your family do for entertainment *away from home?*

_____

_____

_____

_____

Which, if any, of these activities does your child enjoy?

_____

_____

_____

_____

When your child does participate in one of the activities that the family uses for recreation, does he or she participate in a special way, or with special rules, that are only understood by the members of the family? ____ yes ____ no
   If yes, please describe the special adaptations that you have made.

_____

_____

_____

What, if any, are some of the problems you have with your child during vacation (when there is no school)?

_____

_____

_____

What are some of the ideas you have that might make these times easier for your child and you?

_____

_____

_____

What Does Your Child Like?

In this section you will give us a picture of some of the things your child likes and dislikes. Since functional programming is based on the needs and desires of each child, this information is vital to planning the program for your child.

Does your child like to be touched by others? ____ Yes ____No
   If yes, how (i.e., tickling, rubbing)?

_____

_____

If there are any people your child seems to enjoy being with most, who are they?

_____

_____

_____

Are there things that your child especially enjoys?

_____

_____

_____

What are the things, if any, that your child enjoys doing that you would prefer he or she did not do?

_____

_____

What are the things, if any, that your child especially does not like to do?

_____

_____

_____

PART 2

How Does Your Child Communicate?

Communication and social interactions are the most important parts of the IMPACT program. This section gives you the opportunity to tell us how well your child communicates. It also allows us to determine the things that seem to be affecting your child's interactions with others. Be sure to add anything to this section that you feel we should know about how your child communicates with others. If your child does NOT do any of the things asked about in any of these questions, please write N/A on the first line.

How does your child ask for food?

_____

_____

_____

Which foods does he or she request most often?

_____

_____

_____

How does your child ask for something he or she wants to do (e.g., toys, games, TV, music)?

_____

_____

_____

Which toys or activities does he or she request most often?

_____

_____

How does your child ask to do things like go outside, swing, play with a ball, and so forth?

_____

_____

_____

Which activities does he or she request most often?

_____

_____

_____

If these requests are directed toward anyone in particular, who would that be?

_____

How does your child let you know when he or she is hurt or in distress?

_____

_____

_____

Please check all those people from whom your child requests help.

____ Mother   ____ Neighbors

____ Father   ____ Friends (peers)

____ Brother   ____ Strangers

____ Sister   ____ Others _____

How does your child ask for help *to get or do something* (e.g., reach a toy on a shelf, open a heavy door)?

_____

_____

_____

Please check all those people from whom your child asks help to obtain or do something?

____ Mother   ____ Neighbors

____ Father   ____ Friends (peers)

____ Brother   ____ Strangers

____ Sister   ____ Others _____

Will your child seek the help of someone who is not nearby? _____ Yes _____ No

Please check all those people from whom your child will seek help.

_____ Mother   _____ Neighbors

_____ Father   _____ Friends (peers)

_____ Brother   _____ Strangers

_____ Sister   _____ Others _____

How does your child ask for help to *find something* at a store, mall, theater, and so forth?

_____

_____

Will your child ask directions from someone he or she does not know? _____ Yes _____ No

How does your child let you know when he or she does *not want* to do some *activity?*

_____

_____

Which *activities* does your child most often *not* want to do?

_____

_____

_____

How does your child let you know when he or she does *not* want *something?*

_____

_____

Which things does your child refuse most often?

_____

_____

How does your child *respond* when someone else comes up to him or her and starts a conversation? If your child responds in more than one way, please list each way.

_____

_____

_____

_____

_____

Please check all those people to whom your child will respond.

_____ Mother   _____ Neighbors

_____ Father   _____ Friends (peers)

_____ Brother   _____ Strangers

_____ Sister   _____ Others _____

How does your child *initiate* contact with other people? If he or she *initiates* contact in more than one way, please list each way below.

_____

_____

_____

Please check all those people with whom your child will *initiate* conversation or other interaction.

_____ Mother   _____ Neighbors

_____ Father   _____ Friends (peers)

_____ Brother   _____ Strangers

_____ Sister   _____ Others _____

How does your child *continue conversation or other interaction* after it has been started by someone else? If your child uses more than one way, please list each below.

_____

_____

_____

_____

Please check all those people with whom your child will *continue a conversation or other social contact.*

_____ Mother   _____ Neighbors

_____ Father   _____ Friends (peers)

_____ Brother   _____ Strangers

_____ Sister   _____ Others _____

How does your child maintain conversation or other contact when he or she has started the interaction?

_____

_____

_____

How does your child ask for rewards, affection, and so forth?

_____

_____

Whom does he or she ask most often?

_____

_____

How does your child ask for comfort when injured or otherwise distressed?

_____

_____

_____

Whom does your child most often seek out for comfort?

_____

_____

_____

Does your child express an interest in his or her surroundings by requesting things by name (e.g., pointing or holding up an object) or by asking questions (e.g., what, how, or why questions)?

_____

_____

_____

_____

a. Will your child ask about his or her surroundings in places less familiar to him or her? _____ Yes _____ No

If yes, please explain. _____

_____

_____

b. Will your child ask about his or her surroundings from people less familiar to him or her? _____ Yes _____ No

If yes, please explain. _____

_____

_____

Does your child ever try to tell you about things he or she has done when you were not there? (Your child will need a considerable amount of some form of language to exhibit this skill.) _____ Yes _____ No

If yes, please explain. _____

_____

_____

_____

a. Does your child attempt to share his or her experiences with people less familiar to him or her as a means of having a conversation or holding their attention? ____ Yes ____ No

If yes, please explain. _____

_____

_____

b. Even if your child is in surroundings that are unfamiliar, will your child still share any experiences he or she might have had? ____ Yes ____ No

If yes, please explain. _____

_____

_____

Does your child play act or pretend? ____ Yes ____ No

If yes, please explain. _____

_____

_____

_____

PART 3

How Well Does Your Child Handle Changes?

Many children with moderate to severe handicaps, especially children with autism, have difficulty changing tasks or dealing with changes in routines or schedules. This section tells us how well your child does with interruptions and unscheduled changes in his or her everyday experiences.

How does your child respond when interrupted by *someone he or she knows?*

_____

_____

_____

How does your child respond when interrupted by *someone he or she does not know?*

_____

_____

_____

Does the way your child deals with interruptions vary with different tasks or activities? ____ Yes ____No

If yes, please explain. _____

_____

How does your child respond when *something* outside your control (e.g., power outage, TV program preempted, car breaks down, store closed unexpectedly) interrupts him or her?

_____

_____

How does this vary with different tasks or activities?

_____

_____

If nothing interrupts your child, will he or she end a task when it is completed, or continue working?

_____

_____

How does this vary with different tasks or activities?

_____

_____

If you tell your child that a change is coming, how does that affect his or her reaction to change? _____

_____

_____

What Does Your Child Do During Leisure Time?

A good portion of the day is spent in recreational or leisure activities. As we become adults, a major task that faces all of us is deciding what we are going to do with our free time and how we can structure our lives so that we can spend that time productively. This section gives us the information we need to be able to begin developing effective recreational and leisure programs for your child.

How does your child occupy himself or herself (i.e., play) independently?

_____

For how long? _____

With which toys or activities? _____

_____

_____

When your child plays with other children, which toys or activities do they use?

_____

_____

Will your child seek out activities to occupy himself or herself independently?
____ Yes   ____No

If a particular activity or object is not available to your child, will he or she seek
out other things to do? ____ Yes   ____No

What are some of the activities that your child likes to do on a regular basis?

_____

_____

What are some of the activities that you would like your child to be able to learn
how to do?

Alone _____

_____

With other people _____

_____

What Can Your Child Do Independently?

One of the main objectives of the IMPACT program is to help children with
autism and other handicaps, moderate to severe, to learn to function as independently as possible. The training required to reach this goal must start earlier than
it does for other children. This section will tell us which skills your child currently
has, and which skills you would like us to work on next.

For each of the following self-help skills, please check "independently" if
your child does not require any assistance or supervision to complete the tasks in
the routine, "yes" if your child can complete the routine with assistance, "no" if
the child does not do the routine (e.g., child tantrums, you do it for him or her).

There may be several tasks that you want your child to learn that are not included on this list. If you identify one or more tasks that your child can do, or that
you would like your child to learn how to do, add them to the list in the spaces
provided at the end of this section.

Can your child prepare a snack or simple meal (e.g., getting some fruit, getting a
sandwich or drink)?

____ Independently

____ Yes, but needs help (describe) _____

_____

____ No (explain) _____

_____

Can your child complete mealtime tasks (i.e., serving food/drink, using utensils):

_____ Independently

_____ Yes, but needs help (describe) _____

_____

_____ No (explain) _____

_____

Can your child clean up after meals (i.e., clear table, wash/dry dishes):

_____ Independently

_____ Yes, but needs help (describe)_____

_____

_____ No (explain) _____

_____

Can your child handle toileting by himself or herself (i.e., gets to/from bathroom, washes/drys hands):

_____ Independently

_____ Yes, but needs help (describe) _____

_____

_____ No (explain)_____

_____

Can your child complete hygiene tasks (i.e., washes/dries hair, brushes teeth):

_____ Independently

_____ Yes, but needs help (describe) _____

_____

_____ No (explain)_____

_____

Can your child *undress* himself or herself:

_____ Independently

_____ Yes, but needs help (describe) _____

_____

_____ No (explain) _____

_____

_____

Can your child *dress* himself or herself:

____ Independently

____ Yes, but needs help (describe) _____

_____

_____

____ No (explain) _____

_____

_____

Can your child wash his or her clothes (i.e., sort clothes, load machine):

____ Independently

____ Yes, but needs help (describe) _____

_____

_____

____ No (explain) _____

_____

_____

Can your child dry his or her clothes (i.e., load and start machine):

____ Independently

____ Yes, but needs help (describe) _____

_____

_____

____ No (explain) _____

_____

_____

Another task that my child *can do* that you did not list is:

_____

_____

Currently, he or she can do it:

____ Independently

____ With some help (describe) _____

_____

_____

Another task that my child *can do* that you did not list is:

_____

_____

Currently, he or she can do it:

____ Independently

____ With some help (describe) _____

_____

_____

A task that I would like my child *to learn* is:

_____

_____

Currently he or she:

____ Can do it with some help (describe) _____

_____

____ Cannot do it at all

A task that I would like my child *to learn* is:

_____

_____

Currently he or she:

____ Can do part of it with some help (describe) _____

_____

____ Cannot do it at all

Now that you have completed the inventory, go back and circle those skills that you consider to be the most important priorities in planning an educational program for your child for the next year or so. Once you have circled the priorities, please list below the five most critical skills you think your child should learn in the next year.

   1. _____

   2. _____

   3. _____

   4. _____

   5. _____

IMPACT HOME AND
COMMUNITY ENVIRONMENT SUMMARY SHEET

Name _____   Date:_____

Check each environment listed on the Home and Community Inventory. Next to each item checked indicate the level of supervision required.

Environments participated in	Inde-pendent	Family adults	Family siblings	Adults others
Outside				
____ Yard (fenced)				
____ Yard (open)				
____ Neighborhood				
____ Park				
____ School yard				
____ Other _____				
_____				
_____				
Community				
____ Campground				
____ Day camp				
____ Overnight camp				
____ Pool				
____ Restaurants				
____ Grocery store				
____ House of worship				
____ Department store				
____ Drug store				
____ Shopping mall				
____ Theater				
____ Other _____				
_____				
_____				

SAMPLE

IMPACT HOME AND
COMMUNITY COMMUNICATION SUMMARY SHEET

Name _____ Date:_____

Check each communicative function listed in the Home and Community Inventory. Next to each function list the form that is most often used to fulfill the function. Finally, list the person(s) to whom the communication is most often directed.

Communicative function	Form	Person(s)
_____ Ask, food		
_____ Ask, activity		
_____ Ask, outside		
_____ Indicate injury		
_____ Help, get things		
_____ Help, find things		
_____ Help, do something		
_____ Ask directions		
_____ Protest, activity		
_____ Protest, food		
_____ Protest, object		
_____ Respond, family		
_____ Respond, adults		
_____ Respond, peers		
_____ Initiate interaction, family		
_____ Initiate interaction, adults		
_____ Initiate interaction, peers		
_____ Continue interaction, family		
_____ Continue interaction, adults		
_____ Continue interaction, peers		
_____ Seek affection		
_____ Seek reward		
_____ Express interest		
_____ Relate past events		
_____ Pretend, fantasy		

IMPACT HOME AND
COMMUNITY PREFERENCE SUMMARY SHEET

Name _____   Date:_____

*List each preference shown on the Home and Community Inventory in the appropriate
spaces in the left hand column. Next, indicate the level of supervision required for each
item.*

Activity		Inde-pendent	Family adults	Family siblings	Adults others
Toys		Inde-pendent	Family adults	Family siblings	Adults others
Games	Modified[1] yes/no	Inde-pendent	Family adults	Family siblings	Adults others

[1]Indication for whether or not game was modified to adapt to child.

IMPACT HOME AND COMMUNITY
PREFERENCE SUMMARY SHEET (continued)

Name _____   Date:_____

Special people: List anyone whom the child seems to seek out more often. Include the activity and situation in which this occurs. Also, if someone can evoke exceptional performance(s), note the circumstances here.

Foods: List any foods that the child especially likes or dislikes.	Likes	Dislikes

Things to avoid: List any particular activity, toy, game, or action that should be avoided initially until you can program effective alternatives.

IMPACT HOME AND
COMMUNITY PROBLEMS SUMMARY SHEET

Name _____   Date:_____

List all the problems shown on the Home and Community Inventory in the left hand column. Next to each problem list the setting, persons involved, and any particulars about the task(s) required or command(s) given.

Problem(s)	Setting	Persons	Tasks/Commands

SAMPLE

C ⟩ IMPACT
Environmental Inventory for School and Community

appendix

PART 1

INVENTORY for _____

Sex _____ Age _____ School _____

Classroom Information

Teacher's name: _____

School address: _____

City _____ State _____ Zip _____

Telephone: (Home): (   )   -   (School): (   )   -

Where Does Your Student Go?

One of the main parts of your student's program is to increase the number of places where he or she can go. This part of the questionnaire tells us about the places you and your class visit and how well your student does in different places with different people and gives you an opportunity to list specific problems your student has in various situations.

How often does your child play outside?

_____ Frequently   _____ Occasionally   _____ Never

Where does your student usually play when outside? If your student plays in more than one place on a *regular* basis, please tell us about how much time is spent in each place.

In protected courtyard? _____ Hrs. _____

Is your yard or playground fenced? _____ Yes _____ No

In areas outside playground or courtyard? _____ Hrs. _____

In a park or neighborhood area near school? _____ Hrs. _____

When your student does play outside, how much supervision does he or she require? (*Check all that apply.*)

_____ My student can play independently

_____ Alone

_____ With other children

_____ My student will play with help from aides or teachers

_____ My student will play with help from other children in my class

_____ My student will play with help from other children in the school

_____ My student will play outside with help from family members

_____ My student will play outside with help from friends or neighbors

What types of problems, if any, does your student present when playing outside (e.g., runs away, tears at plants and eats them, hits other children, runs out into traffic)?

_____

_____

_____

Which community/recreation settings does your student use?

_____

_____

_____

When your student goes to a community recreation setting, what amount of direct supervision is required? (*Check all that apply.*)

_____ None (independent)

_____ With other students in the class

_____ With teacher or aide

_____ With family members

_____ With friends or neighbors

Do you regularly use these environments as part of the regular school day?

_____ Yes _____ No

If you do not use these places on a regular basis, how often does your class frequent these places?

_____ Almost never _____ Once a quarter _____ Once a month

What community services (e.g., restaurants, stores, house of worship) does your student use?

_____

_____

_____

_____

When your student does use community services, what level of direct supervision is required? (*Check all the apply.*)

_____ None (independent)

_____ With other members of the class

_____ Teachers and/or aides

_____ With family members

_____ With friends or neighbors

Do you use these places regularly as part of the school day?

_____ Yes _____ No

If you do not use these places on a regular basis, how often does your class frequent these places?

_____ Almost never _____ Once a quarter _____ Once a month

Are there places that you or other members of your class go where you usually would not take your student?

_____ Yes _____ No

If yes, where? _____

_____

_____

What problems are created when he or she does go along?

_____

_____

_____

What skills does your student need to learn before you would feel comfortable letting him or her go *with you* on a regular basis? If the problems are different in different situations, please list each separately. (*Attach a separate sheet if you need more space.*)

_____

_____

_____

_____

_____

What skills would your student have to learn to be able to go to these places *alone*? If the skills needed are different in different situations, please list each separately. (*Attach a separate sheet if you need more space.*)

_____

_____

_____

_____

_____

Does your student like to ride on the bus? ____ Yes ____ No

What problems occur, if any, when he or she has to ride:

5–15 minutes _____

_____

15 minutes or more _____

_____

What Does Your Student Do Most of the Time?

This section is designed to give you an idea about the number and types of activities your student participates in during the week. You will need to note where, when, and with whom your student interacts. You will especially want to know the problems you and your student face on a day-to-day basis. Be sure to add any additional comments you feel will help describe what goes on during a typical week. This information will be used to aid in designing a functional program for your student.

What does your student usually do between being dropped off at school and entering the classroom?

_____

_____

_____

Which of those activities does your student do:

Independently _____

With a teacher and/or aide _____

_____

With someone else (e.g., bus driver, parent) _____

_____

What special problems, if any, occur during those times?

_____

_____

_____

What does your student usually do between entering the class and your first organized activity?

_____

_____

_____

Which of those activities does your student do:

Independently _____

With a teacher and/or aide _____

_____

With someone else (e.g., bus driver, parent) _____

_____

With other children (peers) _____

_____

What special problems, if any, occur during those times?

_____

_____

_____

What does your student usually do during a typical day? List the general activities and an estimate of how long each activity lasts.

_____

_____

_____

_____

_____

_____

Which of those activities does your student do:

Independently _____

With a teacher and/or aide _____

_____

With someone else (e.g., bus driver, parent) _____

_____

With other children (peers) _____

_____

What special problems, if any, occur during those times?

_____

_____

_____

Does your student play with other children? _____ Yes _____ No

> If yes, with whom (i.e., peers in class, other peers from school, neighborhood children, siblings)?

> _____

> _____

> _____

When your student does participate in one of the activities that the class uses for recreation or reward, does he or she participate in a special way, or with special rules, that are only understood by the members of the class or by the teaching staff? _____ Yes _____ No

> If yes, please describe the special adaptations that you have made.

> _____

> _____

> _____

Are vacation times (when there is no school) a difficult time for your student and/or his or her parents?

> _____ Yes _____ No

> If yes, what are some of the problems?

> _____

> _____

> _____

What are some of the ideas you have that might make these times easier for your student and his or her family?

> _____

> _____

> _____

What Does Your Student Like?

> *In this section you will describe some of the things your student likes and dislikes. Since functional programming is based on the needs and desires of each student, this information is vital to planning the program for your student.*

Does your student like to be touched by others? _____ Yes _____ No

> If yes, how (i.e., tickling, rubbing)?

> _____

> _____

If there are any people your student seems to enjoy being with most at school, who are they?

> _____

> _____

Are there things that your student especially enjoys?

> _____

> _____

> _____

What are the things, if any, that your student enjoys doing that you would prefer he or she did not do?

_____

_____

_____

What are the things, if any, that your student especially does not like to do?

_____

_____

_____

Who are the people, if any, that your student does not like?

_____

_____

_____

What are the particular situations, if any, in which your student seems to be more displeased or dissatisfied?

_____

_____

_____

PART 2

How Does Your Student Communicate?

Communication and social interactions are the most important parts of the IMPACT program. This section gives you the opportunity to tell us how well your student communicates. It also allows you to determine the things that seem to be affecting your student's interactions with others. Be sure to add anything to this section that you feel helps explain how your student communicates with others. If your student does NOT do any of the things asked about in any of these questions, please write N/A on the first line.

How does your student ask for food?

_____

_____

_____

Which foods does he or she request most often?

_____

_____

_____

How does your student ask for something he or she wants to do (e.g., toys, games, TV, music)?

_____

_____

_____

Which toys or activities does he or she request most often?

_____

_____

_____

How does your student ask to do things like go outside, swing, play with a ball, and so forth?

_____

_____

_____

Which activities does he or she request most often?

_____

_____

_____

If these requests are directed toward anyone in particular, who would that be?

_____

How does your student let you know when he or she is hurt or in distress?

_____

_____

_____

Please check all those people from whom your student requests help.

_____ Teacher	_____ Aide
_____ Other students in class	_____ Other students in school
_____ Mother	_____ Neighbors
_____ Father	_____ Friends (peers)
_____ Brother	_____ Strangers
_____ Sister	_____ Others _____

How does your student ask for help *to get or do something* (e.g., reach a toy on a shelf, open a heavy door)?

_____

_____

_____

Please check all those people from whom your student asks help to obtain or do something.

_____ Teacher	_____ Aide
_____ Other students in class	_____ Other students in school
_____ Mother	_____ Neighbors
_____ Father	_____ Friends (peers)
_____ Brother	_____ Strangers
_____ Sister	_____ Others _____

Will your student seek the help of someone who is not nearby? _____ Yes _____ No
Please check all those people from whom your student will seek help.

_____ Teacher	_____ Aide
_____ Other students in class	_____ Other students in school
_____ Mother	_____ Neighbors
_____ Father	_____ Friends (peers)
_____ Brother	_____ Strangers
_____ Sister	_____ Others _____

How does your student ask for help to *find something* at a store, mall, theater, and so forth?

_____

_____

Will your student ask directions from someone he or she does not know? _____ Yes
_____ No

How does your student let you know when he or she does *not* want to do some *activity*?

_____

_____

    Which *activities* does your student most often *not* want to do?

    _____

    _____

    _____

How does your student let you know when he or she does *not* want *something*?

_____

_____

    Which things does your student refuse most often?

    _____

    _____

How does your student *respond* when someone else comes up to him or her and starts a conversation? If your student responds in more than one way, please list each way.

_____

_____

_____

_____

    Please check all those people to whom your student will respond.

_____ Teacher	_____ Aide
_____ Other students in class	_____ Other students in school
_____ Mother	_____ Neighbors
_____ Father	_____ Friends (peers)
_____ Brother	_____ Strangers
_____ Sister	_____ Others _____

How does your student *initiate* contact with other people? If he or she *initiates* contact in more than one way, please list each way below.

_____

_____

_____

_____

    Please check all those people with whom your student will *initiate* conversation or other interaction.

_____ Teacher	_____ Aide
_____ Other students in class	_____ Other students in school
_____ Mother	_____ Neighbors
_____ Father	_____ Friends (peers)

_____ Brother   _____ Strangers

_____ Sister   _____ Others _____

How does your student *continue conversation or other interaction* after it has been started by someone else? If your student uses more than one way, please list each below.

_____

_____

_____

Please check all those people with whom your student will *continue a conversation or other social contact.*

_____ Teacher   _____ Aide

_____ Other students in class   _____ Other students in school

_____ Mother   _____ Neighbors

_____ Father   _____ Friends (peers)

_____ Brother   _____ Strangers

_____ Sister   _____ Others _____

How does your student maintain conversation or other contact when he or she has started the interaction?

_____

_____

_____

How does your student ask for rewards, affection, and so forth?

_____

_____

Whom does he or she ask most often?

_____

_____

How does your student ask for comfort when injured or otherwise distressed?

_____

_____

_____

Whom does he or she most often seek out for comfort?

_____

_____

_____

Does your student express an interest in his or her surroundings by requesting things by name (e.g., pointing or holding up an object) or by asking questions (e.g., what, how, or why questions)?

_____

_____

_____

a. Will your student ask about his or her surroundings in places less familiar to him or her? _____ Yes _____ No

If yes, please explain. _____
_____
_____

b. Will your student ask about his or her surroundings from people less familiar to him or her? ____ Yes ____ No
If yes, please explain. _____
_____
_____

Does your student ever try to tell you about things he or she has done when you were not there? (Your student will need a considerable amount of some form of language to exhibit this skill.) ____ Yes ____ No
If yes, please explain. _____
_____
_____
_____

a. Does your student attempt to share his or her experiences with people less familiar to him or her as a means of having a conversation or holding their attention? ____ Yes ____ No
If yes, please explain. _____
_____

b. Even if your child is in surroundings that are unfamiliar, will he or she still share any experiences he or she might have had? ____ Yes ____ No
If yes, please explain. _____
_____

Does your student play act or pretend? ____ Yes ____ No
If yes, please explain. _____
_____
_____
_____

PART 3

How Well Does Your Student Handle Changes?

Many children with moderate to severe handicaps, especially children with autism, have difficulty changing tasks or dealing with changes in routines or schedules. This section describes how well your student does with interruptions and unscheduled changes in his or her everyday experiences.

How does your student respond when interrupted by *someone he or she knows?*
_____
_____
_____

How does your student respond when interrupted by *someone he or she does not know?*

_____

_____

_____

Does the way your student deals with interruptions vary with different tasks or activities?
_____ Yes _____No

    If yes, please explain. _____

_____

_____

How does your student respond when *something* outside your control (e.g., power outage, TV program preempted, car breaks down, store closed unexpectedly) interrupts him or her?

_____

_____

How does this vary with different tasks or activities?

_____

_____

If nothing interrupts your student, will he or she end a task when it is completed, or continue working?

_____

_____

How does this vary with different tasks or activities?

_____

_____

If you tell your student that a change is coming, how does that affect his or her reaction to change? _____

_____

_____

What Does Your Student Do During Leisure Time?

A good portion of the day is spent in recreational or leisure activities. As we become adults, a major task that faces all of us is deciding what we are going to do with our free time and how we can structure our lives so that we can spend that time productively. This section provides the information needed to be able to begin developing effective recreational and leisure programs for your student.

How does your student occupy himself or herself (i.e., play) independently?

_____

_____

    For how long? _____

    With which toys or activities? _____

_____

_____

When your student plays with other children, which toys or activities do they use?

_____

_____

_____

Will your student seek out activities to occupy himself or herself independently? _____ Yes _____No

If a particular activity or object is not available to your student, will he or she seek out other things to do? _____ Yes _____No

What are some of the activities that your student likes to do on a regular basis?

_____

_____

_____

What are some of the activities that you would like your student to be able to learn how to do:

Alone _____

_____

_____

With other people _____

_____

_____

What Can Your Student Do Independently?

One of the main objectives of the IMPACT program is to help children with autism and other handicaps, moderate to severe, to learn to function as independently as possible. The training required to reach this goal must start earlier than it does for other children. This section will list those skills your student currently has, and which skills you think should be worked on next. You will compare this list with the one created by the parents to develop your independence/self-help programs.

For each of the following self-help skills, please check "independently" if your student does not require any assistance or supervision to complete the tasks in the routine, "yes" if your student can complete the routine with assistance, "no" if your student does not do the routine (e.g., student tantrums, you do it for him or her).

There may be several tasks that you want your student to learn that are not included on this list. If you identify one or more tasks that your student can do, or that you would like your student to learn how to do, add them to the list in the spaces provided at the end of this section.

Can your student prepare a snack or simple meal (e.g., getting some fruit, getting a sandwich or drink)?

_____ Independently

_____ Yes, but needs help (describe) _____

_____

_____

_____

_____ No (explain) _____

_____

_____

Can your student complete mealtime tasks (i.e., serving food/drink, using utensils):

_____ Independently

_____ Yes, but needs help (describe) _____

_____

_____

_____ No (explain) _____

_____

_____

Can your student clean up after meals (i.e., clear table, wash/dry dishes):

_____ Independently

_____ Yes, but needs help (describe)_____

_____

_____

_____ No (explain) _____

_____

_____

Can your student handle toileting by himself or herself (i.e., gets to/from bathroom, washes/drys hands):

_____ Independently

_____ Yes, but needs help (describe) _____

_____

_____

_____ No (explain)_____

_____

_____

Can your student complete hygiene tasks (i.e., washes/dries hair, brushes teeth):

_____ Independently

_____ Yes, but needs help (describe) _____

_____

_____

_____ No (explain)_____

_____

_____

Can your student *undress* himself or herself:

_____ Independently

_____ Yes, but needs help (describe) _____

_____

_____

_____ No (explain) _____

_____

_____

Can your student *dress* himself or herself:

_____ Independently

_____ Yes, but needs help (describe) _____

_____

_____

_____ No (explain) _____

_____

_____

Can your student wash his or her clothes (i.e., sort clothes, load machine):

_____ Independently

_____ Yes, but needs help (describe) _____

_____

_____

_____ No (explain) _____

_____

_____

Can your student dry his or her clothes (i.e., load and start machine):

_____ Independently

_____ Yes, but needs help (describe) _____

_____

_____

_____ No (explain) _____

_____

_____

Another task(s) that my student can do *independently* is:

_____

_____

_____

Another task(s) that my student can do *with some help* is:

_____

_____

_____

A task that I would like my student *to learn* is: _____

_____

_____

Currently he or she:

_____ Can do it with some help (describe) _____

_____

_____ Cannot do it at all

A task that I would like my student *to learn* is: _____

_____

Currently he or she:

_____ Can do part of it with some help (describe) _____

_____

_____ Cannot do it at all

Now that you have completed the inventory, go back and circle those skills that you con-sider to be the most important priorities in planning an educational program for your stu-dent for the next year or so. Once you have circled the priorities, please list below the five most critical skills *you think your student should learn in the next year. These skills, when combined with the priorities selected by the student's parents, will form the basis for your functional programming for your student.*

1. _____

2. _____

3. _____

4. _____

5. _____

IMPACT SCHOOL AND
COMMUNITY ENVIRONMENT SUMMARY SHEET

Name: _____ Date: _____

Check each environment shown on the School and Community Inventory. Next to each item checked indicate the level of supervision required.

Environments participated in	Inde-pendent	Adults	Peers class	Peers others
Outside				
___ Yard (fenced)				
___ Yard (open)				
___ Neighborhood				
___ Park				
___ School yard				
___ Other _____				
_____				
_____				
Community				
___ Campground				
___ Day camp				
___ Overnight camp				
___ Pool				
___ Restaurants				
___ Grocery store				
___ House of worship				
___ Department store				
___ Drug store				
___ Shopping mall				
___ Theater				
___ Other _____				
_____				
_____				

IMPACT SCHOOL AND
COMMUNITY COMMUNICATION SUMMARY SHEET

Name: _____   Date: _____

Check each communicative function shown on the School and Community Inventory. Next to each function list the form that is most often used to fulfill the function. Finally, list the person(s) to whom the communication is most often directed.

Communicative function	Form	Person(s)
____ Ask, food		
____ Ask, activity		
____ Ask, outside		
____ Indicate injury		
____ Help, get things		
____ Help, find things		
____ Help, do something		
____ Ask directions		
____ Protest, activity		
____ Protest, food		
____ Protest, object		
____ Respond, family		
____ Respond, adults		
____ Respond, peers		
____ Initiate interaction, family		
____ Initiate interaction, adults		
____ Initiate interaction, peers		
____ Continue interaction, family		
____ Continue interaction, adults		
____ Continue interaction, peers		
____ Seek affection		
____ Seek reward		
____ Express interest		
____ Relate past events		
____ Pretend, fantasy		

IMPACT SCHOOL AND
COMMUNITY PREFERENCE SUMMARY SHEET

Name: _____ Date: _____

List each preference shown on the School and Community Inventory in the appropriate spaces in the left hand column. Next, indicate the level of supervision required for each item.

Activity	Inde-pendent	Adults	Peers class	Peers others

Toys	Inde-pendent	Adults	Peers class	Peers others

Games	Modified[1] yes/no	Inde-pendent	Adults	Peers class	Peers others

[1]Indication for whether or not game was modified to adapt to child.

IMPACT SCHOOL AND COMMUNITY
PREFERENCE SUMMARY SHEET (continued)

Name: _____   Date: _____

Special people: List anyone whom the child seems to seek out more often. Include the activity and situation in which this occurs. Also, if someone can evoke exceptional performance(s), note the circumstances here.

Foods: List any foods that the child especially likes or dislikes.	Likes	Dislikes

Things to avoid: List any particular activity, toy, game, or action that should be avoided initially until you can program effective alternatives.

IMPACT SCHOOL AND
COMMUNITY PROBLEMS SUMMARY SHEET

Name: _____   Date: _____

List all the problems shown on the School and Community Inventory in the left hand column. Next to each problem list the setting, persons involved, and any particulars about the task(s) required or command(s) given.

Problem(s)	Setting	Persons	Tasks/Commands

SAMPLE

D ⟩ A Parent Guide to Understanding the IMPACT Curriculum

appendix

The IMPACT curriculum, which was developed specifically to help children and youth with moderate to severe handicaps, is designed to teach your child the skills he or she needs to function or do activities at home and in other places outside home, both now and in the future. Those who use the IMPACT program believe that the people working with these students *must* work with their parents too. Parents, after all, have the best understanding of their children! Information you give us, therefore, is necessary to the development of an appropriate (fitting for the child's age and needs), functional (useful), educational program for your child. This handbook explains how you can help and what the teachers will be doing.

For many years, there were very few educational services for children with moderate to severe handicaps. Although there have been special education classrooms since the early 1900s, students used to be required to have certain basic skills to be admitted. Children who were not very social, did not communicate well, could not use the toilet by themselves, could not move themselves about, or who behaved in ways that were very hard to deal with were often left out of school programs. In the 1950s parents began to take strong action and, mostly because of that action, PL 94-142, the Education for All Handicapped Children Act, was signed into law in 1975. That law established the right of every child, no matter how severe his or her disability, to a free, appropriate public education. At the time PL 94-142 was passed, however, many children were still not learning the skills needed to function outside of school. Because of this, teachers and others involved in education have recently begun to concentrate on teaching students skills that people need to use in day-to-day living. We call these skills *functional skills*.

IMPACT is a functional curriculum that allows students to participate in home and community activities as much as possible. If your child is going to learn to function in different everyday places, he or she will need to learn many different skills. For example, children are unlikely to enjoy going to the park if they cannot use any of the playground equipment or participate in other recreational activities. They will not be able to ride a bus by themselves if they do not know which bus to take, when to take it, how to pay their fare, and how to get along with other riders. If children do not learn a wide range of skills, they will always need someone else to take care of the different things they need in daily living. Because you know best what your child needs to learn for daily living, we need you to be part of the IMPACT way of teaching to make sure that the most useful (functional) skills are taught.

IMPACT IS A PROCESS

IMPACT is a curriculum that teaches children using a process. The process begins with the Environmental Inventories. Each inventory is a full list of questions. There is one inventory for school, which the teacher will fill out, and another for home, which we will ask you to fill out. We use the inventories for two reasons: 1) to understand which skills your child needs to learn so he or she can participate more fully in home and outside of home activities, and 2) to put together priority (the most important) goals for your child's individualized education program (IEP). The IEP is the learning plan put together especially for your individual child only. The inventories are divided into two main sections. In Part 1, we ask about where your child goes, what he or she does most of the time, and what he or she likes. Part 2 asks you to tell about the ways in which your child communicates, how well he or she handles changes, what he or she does during free time, and the degree to which he or she can do self-help skills (help himself or herself) independently. Of course, the areas covered in the inventories overlap. They are separated in the inventories simply to help you and the teacher organize your answers. When your child's program is put together, the areas will be combined into activities that normally occur at home, school, and in the community.

WHAT THE INVENTORIES DO

Tell How Much Help/Supervision Your Child Needs

The IMPACT Environmental Inventories for Home and Community and for School and Community tell what your child needs to learn and what he or she can already do. For some skills, your child may need a lot of help; for other skills, you may only need to say something to get your child started or, he or she may not need help. It is important to know how much help and supervision your child needs before we start teaching.

Tell How Your Child Communicates

All behaviors have two components (parts): form and function. Looking at these two parts helps us understand how communication works. Function can be described as what your child is trying to tell you (the *purpose* of the behavior). Forms are the *ways* your child tells you (the behavior itself). For example, one of the earliest functions children develop is getting what they want (function). They can do this by crying, reaching towards something, pointing, or saying, "I am hungry, can I have a sandwich?" (forms). The inventory will help show which functions your child has and the forms she or he uses. This information, in turn, will help us put together communication programs that will be most useful to your child.

Tell the Different Environments Your Child Goes To

The various situations and places your child will be in, or is likely to be in later, should also be listed in the inventory. When filling out the inventory, think about both what your child needs now and his or her needs in the 2 or 3 years to come. Your child may not have the skills needed in a place you want to visit (e.g., shopping mall, fast food restaurant, grandparents' home), so you will want to list both the skills and the places that are important to you. In addition, your child may have behavior problems that cause great problems for your family. Those concerns should also be listed on the inventory.

The Home and Community Environmental Inventory is designed so you can provide the educational team with information about what kinds of things you want to be part of your child's education. The priority (most important) areas you select will form the basis for your child's program. The teacher will complete the School and Community Environmental Inventory, and the two inventories will be combined when the IEP is written.

THE IEP PROCESS

IEP goals (what your child needs to learn) show up in the completed inventories. Learning the most important skills for your child makes the next step of forming IEP goals much easier. After completing the inventory, you should circle the skills you consider important for your child to learn first. There is a space for you to list what you think are the five most important skills of all.

There may be more priority skills than there is time to teach. How, then, do we decide what your child needs to learn and when that learning needs to occur? Since functional skills are skills that are longitudinal (useful all through the child's life), age-appropriate (right for the child's age), and useful in many places, what we teach your child should be, too. Longitudinal skills include, for example, communicating, using the toilet, dressing, and preparing meals. Age-appropriate skills make it more possible for your child to spend time with other children the same age who are nonhandicapped. If a child is 12 years old, learning to ride a bicycle is more fitting than learning to ride a tricycle because average children of 12 ride bicycles and would spend more time with other bicycle-riding children than with those on tricycles. Also, bicycle riding is a skill that will be useful even when your child is an adult. The same is true of learning to use music equipment (e.g., a stereo, tape recorder, radios). Almost everyone listens to music; it is the type of music that changes as we grow older. Finally, skills that can be used in several different situations and places are more useful than those that can be used only in one. Using the toilet, carrying on a conversation, and riding a bus, for example, are more important than learning to raise your hand or doing three piece puzzles.

HOW YOUR CHILD WILL BE TAUGHT

Teaching in Natural Contexts

Functional (useful) skills should be taught in their natural contexts; that is, when and where they would normally be used. Think about what people generally do; usually, they have a reason for doing the things they do in a particular situation. Most of us do not do one thing over and over again when there is no purpose. Neither should your child. The skills he or she learns should be taught in a way that pays attention to the purpose of the skill. For example, we usually need to match colors in the real world when we match our socks after doing laundry. Most people do not, however, sit at a table matching a red card with another red card time after time. When sorting socks, we are matching colors for a reason. Many children with moderate to severe handicaps have difficulty knowing the context in which (when and where) to use the skills they have learned. By teaching in natural contexts, the IMPACT program teaches not only how to use skills, but where and when to use them as well.

How Teaching in Context Will be Done: Task Analysis

After educational goals are understood, your child's teacher will do a *task analysis* for each goal. A task analysis (also called a *routine*) is used to break a task down into steps that can be taught individually. The procedure begins by looking at starting and ending steps of the task. The starting step will be a natural cue (something that happens naturally) in the environment that signals the beginning of a task, and the ending step will be the critical effect (what should finally happen as a result of all the steps). For example, a natural cue for the routine of Coming to Dinner may be someone calling you (starting step), and the critical effect is eating (ending step). The natural cue for getting ready for work may be the alarm going off in the morning (starting step), and the critical effect is going to work on time (ending step). Figure 1 is a sample of a Dressing for Gym routine. As you can see, the natural cue is the teacher telling Johnny that it is time for gym, and the critical effect or outcome is going to the gym.

After the task analysis is completed, an *assessment* will be conducted to find out how well your child performs each step of the routine. The assessment, which will look at how your child does the skill at several different times, tells the teacher precisely how much help your child needs to do a particular task successfully and completely. The help required may range from you physically helping your child to move to no help at all.

Natural cue: Teacher says, "Carl, it's time to change for gym."

1. Carl walks to clothes shelf.
2. Carl gets gym clothes from shelf.
3. Carl goes to changing area and sits in chair.
4. Carl takes off shoes.
5. Carl takes off socks and stands up.
6. Carl takes off pants.
7. Carl takes off shirt.
8. Carl puts on gym shirt.
9. Carl puts on gym shorts and sits in chair.
10. Carl puts on gym socks.
11. Carl puts on gym shoes and stands up.
12. Carl picks up clothes.
13. Carl puts clothes in basket.
14. Carl waves "good bye" and goes to gym.

Critical effect: Begin participation in gym activities.

Figure 1. Dressing for Gym routine.

Actual *instructional programming* (teaching) begins after the assessment is completed. The teaching process is slightly different from the assessment process. In the assessment, help is given after allowing the student to try the step on his or her own. During teaching, the type of help that the assessment showed us was needed is given immediately; that is, before the student has a chance to respond on his or her own. If the child does a step with the help that the assessment showed us the child needed, then we say the student did the step correctly. If the child does not do the step with that help, then we say that he or she made an error. As the student is able to do the step better and better, the teacher gives less and less help. Progress, then, is measured by the child being more and more able to do the skill on his or her own. What you will see as your child grows in his or her educational program is that he or she will need less help with each step and will come closer to being able to do the entire routine on his or her own. The method of teaching used in IMPACT has been found to be a highly efficient and effective strategy for helping students to function as independently as they can, and in the least restrictive (most natural) environment possible.

WHAT MORE TO EXPECT

When the program for teaching your child is actually in use, what more can you expect to have to do? This section will explain what we will need you to do once your child's teaching program begins.

Generalization Probes

It is important to teach skills when and where they normally occur. There may be times when this cannot be done at school (e.g., making a snack in the kitchen at home or how to behave in a house of worship). At these times, we may teach in places where your child would use the same kinds of skills (e.g., making a snack at school or attending a school play). To make sure that behaviors taught in school are used in other places, home and community *generalization probes* or tests will be done. A generalization probe is simply a way of telling whether or not the skills learned at school are also used in other places where your child needs them. Your child's teacher will contact you to ask a series of questions about how well your child can do a particular routine or activity. You will be asked to tell how well and how consistently your child does the routine. If he or she has not been doing the skill well enough, you will be asked to describe what your child does instead. If there are differences between what your child does at home and what he or she does at school, the teacher will work to help your child do his or her best in both places. With this type of communication between you at home and the school, we can make sure your child uses skills in as many places as possible.

We May Ask You For More Help

Because the natural place to use some skills is outside of the classroom, some teaching will need to be done off the school grounds. It is possible that your child's teacher will ask you to help when the class goes out by doing the driving, coming with the class, or sending money to school that will be used to help teach your child to purchase the items he or she needs. The specific type of help that we will ask you for depends on what we find out your child needs to learn, and how easy it is to get to some places in the community. Although this may seem like a lot to ask, being able to go out into the community is *critical* to teaching students with moderate to severe handicaps skills that are likely to be useful all through their lives. Anything that you are willing to do will help your child get more practice using important skills in the community.

SPECIAL CONCERNS

The management of children with moderate to severe handicaps (dealing with their problem behaviors) is a problem parents and teachers must face daily. Over the years, many methods have been developed to help you cope with your child's behavior. In order to be successful, you will use different ways to deal with different kinds of problem behaviors. No handbook can tell you everything to do, but ideas can help. Here are a number of ideas that may help you be more effective:

1. If your child's behavior is causing a problem, try to understand why she or he is behaving that way. When faced with a situation you are unsure of, ask yourself,

"What could my child be trying to say to me?" If a child is throwing a tantrum because he or she is trying to ask for help, or is sick, you will handle it differently from the way you will if he or she does not want to do some chore. The point here is that many behaviors we consider unfitting to a situation or disruptive probably have a communicative intent (purpose). Children who know very few appropriate (fitting) ways to communicate may use problem behaviors to show needs, protests, emotions, and so forth when they have no other way to deliver the message. By attempting to see the purpose of your child's behavior, you may be able to deal with the problem in more productive ways than otherwise, and you may be able to give the teacher valuable information that will help to develop more effective behavior management (better ways to deal with problem behavior) and communication programs.

2.   Children tend to repeat things that worked in the past. They will also stop acting a certain way if it does not work or if something else works better. Try to look at the kinds of behaviors that work for your child. Is your child getting rewards like food, toys, activities, attention, and so forth when he or she is acting "nice?" If so, great! But, perhaps some rewards are less obvious or are working against what you want your child to do. Maybe you give in or give up after you have told your child to dress and he or she cries and kicks. This giving up reinforces crying, that is, encourages your child to do it again. Try to reward your child only after he or she does the right thing. It is hard to do, and you will not always succeed, but each time you succeed it will help.

3.   Try to act immediately when you reward or discourage a behavior. This will help your child understand that how you react depends on what he or she is doing.

4.   Try to be as consistent as you can. Of course, this is not always possible; no one can be in all places at all times and no one can give 100% of their attention to the activities of their children. Try, however, not to overlook a problem behavior on some occasions and respond to that same behavior on other occasions. Since perfect consistency on all behavior is probably impossible, try to do this with a small number of behaviors to begin with. You can deal with additional less disruptive behavior later.

5.   Children tend to get tired of particular rewards if you use them too much. Try to use different rewards or give your child a choice. You can also link the learning of new skills with tasks and activities that your child already knows and enjoys. When your child does the new task, you could reward him or her by allowing him or her to do a favorite activity. For example, after using the toilet, a child may be allowed to go play outside or play the piano.

6.   Whatever behaviors you decide to teach, always try to teach them when and where they naturally would be used. Teach communication skills when your child needs to communicate, eating skills during times your child eats, or dressing skills when your child needs to dress or change. If skills are taught at a time when they do not have a purpose, then your child is likely to become bored and/or show problem behaviors.

TALKING TO YOUR CHILD'S TEACHER

In this *Parent Guide* we have described how the IMPACT program works and why you are so important to its success. We believe this program will help you and the school work together in planning your child's education. The IMPACT process will help you give the teacher and other people involved in your child's education information about your child's needs and progress. If you want more detailed information about any parts of the program, please ask the teacher. Through continual communication throughout the year a truly functional (useful) program for your child can be developed.

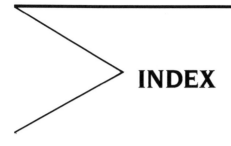

INDEX